Alisa Miller

Understanding Her

Alisa Miller

Copyright © Alice Miller & New Line Publishing, 2010. All rights reserved.

The right of Alice Miller and New Line Publishing to be identified as copyright holders of this work has been asserted in accordance with the Copyright, Designs and Patents Act, 1988.

ISBN 978-1-84481-994-2

This ebook edition published 2010. - Understanding Her.

Published by New Line Publishing, 118 Gatley Road, Cheadle, Cheshire, SK8 4AD, UK.

Find us on the World Wide Web at: www.alisa-miller.com

Editing, cover and interior design by WebDirectStudio
www.webdirectstudio.com (website)
info@webdirectstudio.com (email)

All images are copyright © by their respective owners

The pictures used in this book are for illustrative purposes only. The people in the pictures are not connected with the book, author or publisher and no link or endorsement between any of them and the topic or content is implied, nor should any be assumed.

Notice of Rights
All rights reserved. No part of this publication may be reproduced, stored in a retrieval system, or transmitted, in any form or by any means, electronic, mechanical, photocopying, recording or otherwise, without the prior permission of both the publishers and copyright owner.

This e-book is sold subject to the condition that it shall not, by way of trade or otherwise, be lent, resold, hired out or otherwise circulated without the publisher's prior

Alisa Miller

consent in any form of binding or cover other than that in which it is published and without a similar condition including this condition being imposed on the subsequent purchaser.

Limit of Liability / Disclaimer of Warranty
Whilst the author and publisher have used their best efforts in preparing this publication, they make no representations of warranties with respect to the accuracy or completeness of its contents and specifically disclaim any implied warranties of merchantability or fitness for a particular purpose. No warranty may be created or extended by sales representatives or sales materials. The advice and strategies contained herein may not be suitable for your situation. You should consult with a professional where appropriate. Neither the author nor publisher shall be liable for the use or non-use of the information contained herein. The fact that a website or organization is referred to in this publication as a citation and/or potential source of further information does not mean that the author or publisher endorses the information that the website or organization may provide or recommendations it may make.

License
Purchase of this publication entitles the buyer to keep one copy on his or her computers (when in digital format) that are for personal use and to print out one copy only. The buyer is not permitted to electronically post it, install it or distribute it in a manner that allows access by others.

The scanning, uploading and distributing of this publication via the Internet, or via any other means, without the permission of the publisher, is illegal and punishable by law. Please purchase only authorized electronic editions, and do not participate or encourage electronic piracy of copyrighted materials. Your support of the author's rights is appreciated.

Alisa Miller

ACKNOWLEDGEMENTS

No book is the product of one person alone no matter how it has been written. Conversations, ideas, suggestions and practical help, all go into its making. This book is no exception. I would like to thank for their help Marc Van Riet, Andy Marsh, Antoni Llovera Rubio, Krishna Ramsundar, Red Danfield and the editors at New Line Publishing. Guys, without your help there were times when I would have given the task up without qualms.

Why do we say the things we say? Why do we overreact over small things? Why do we put weight on? Why do we so desperately want you to marry us?

You could never understand us but we know you have been trying really hard. And it's time we explained.

Alisa

Alisa Miller

Chapter 30, verses 18 and 19: Three things there are which are too wonderful for me, four which I do not understand: the way of an eagle in the sky, the way of a serpent on the rock, the way of a ship out at sea, and the way of a man with a woman.

-Proverbs

#1. HER LOOKS: THE BATTLE FOR BEAUTY

Here is a truth you need to know about every woman: We are freaking scared, each one of us. We are scared that tomorrow we will wake up and the scales are going to tell us we've put weight on. We are scared that if we eat a croissant after 6 o'clock the Goddess of Fatness is going to drag us down to hell three minutes later. We are scared of getting older. We are scared that someone else, more beautiful and fresh is going to take you away from us. But we will never tell you that because we are too afraid to show you how really scared we are.

One suffers to be beautiful and modern beauty standards demand a toll of suffering from every one of us. We suffer at the gym, we suffer at lunch time, and we suffer every morning and every night and all the time in between. We try to be slim and we try to

Alisa Miller

follow fashion for as long as our finances can allow us. We will, for example, pay triple the price of a handbag (compared to the 'average' cost for one) if we feel it will make us stand out from the crowd of other women who are trying just as hard as we are. All these ridiculous things we do on a daily basis, all these things you judge us for we do them (most of the time) in order to attract you and feel beautiful.

Every woman lives in fear; sometimes it gets better on a better day when we feel like goddesses spoiled by your attention and sometimes it's really bad and all we want to do is to hide under the covers staying all day in bed. Most of us are insecure. And the better looking a woman is the more insecurity and fear she has got hidden inside of her.

We are never 100% sure we look good and if we make you feel we do it's not for real; we pretend to be indifferent in order to hide our real fear under a mask of overconfidence. We believe that being a bitch is a convenient choice; we pretend that you can't hurt us because we don't care what you think about us. Sure you can, we just won't show you we're hurt. And next day it will start all over again for us.

The world of a woman is fairy complicated. We always fight for beauty; we fight to feel beautiful even if that feeling is going to be brief and we will do anything to experience it (like going on crash diets and trying crazy surgeries). And with the standards of beauty these days pushing against the limit of human ability to fit the parameters (the thinner the better?) we are more likely to fail in our own eyes. When you see a gorgeous woman in the street you can say for sure she is gorgeous because it's exactly what you see. But when she looks in the mirror herself she sees all the imperfections and unreached goals and she hates herself and her failure to reach her ideal self (even though sometimes it is simply not possible and she has totally unreachable goals).

It can get pretty ugly the way she can punish herself for not being perfect. We go hungry, we spend all our money on being beautiful, we would agree to go under the scalpel if we feel it will get us any closer to the ideal we are trying to reach. We can risk our lives on dangerous paths in order to be beautiful. We will sell our souls for beauty without a second thought. For example, we would try an experimental drug if we would think it can, just possibly can, make our breasts a little bigger or our eyelashes a little longer and totally ignore the possibility that there might be serious consequences.

We are all the same when it comes to beauty - truly mad; some of us more, some of us less. And it all comes from insecurity and the fear of being alone. We are programmed by nature to find the right partner and the more we attract the better choice we will have. We feel the pressure of competition and with the development of the media tricks and airbrushing we feel that we can never compete with all these celebrities and top models. We try, we fight, we fail and we rise again.

And each one of us has a hungry ego that needs constant feeding so we can fear less and be more confident. That's why we dress up, we pay for implants, and we even smoke just to stay slim so that once we leave the house we can see your heads turn when we pass by. And yes we always see when you do that. And count every time you do. We score points to boost our egos.

A woman's ego is a powerful thing. We will fight for your attention when we are not even interested in you as a partner or as a lover. But if someone else is interested, some other woman, we will flirt and play just to prove to ourselves that we can have you and that the other woman can't. We fight to be the one you notice in the crowd. But as we all do the same thing competing with each other is getting tougher and the ways to get to be the "better looking one" are getting more and more extreme.

If you don't tell a woman you care for that she looks great and she is beautiful she will find someone else who will. Because she needs it just as much as you need to masturbate. A woman has a natural thirst for being appreciated. She needs to feel she is wanted. And never assume that she knows that she is beautiful anyway. Today she knows it and tomorrow she already has doubts. It doesn't take much from you if you tell her she looks fabulous every so often but it makes a huge difference to her. It makes her happy. It will make any woman happy.

It's a common thing a lot of guys may say: "my wife used to be beautiful before we got married." And it will probably be true. A lot of girls try really hard to be beautiful in order to find a husband and once they do they, well, relax a little and let themselves go. But it's not all their fault. Marriage for every woman means security, the ultimate promise from a man to be there for her for the rest of her life. And this is the greatest fear of every woman - to be alone and not being able to find anyone to share her life with. So naturally when the promise is made she doesn't feel that she has to try as hard anymore and she finally concentrates on other things like household and children or her career.

Once again it's not entirely her fault when it happens. A woman needs to feel that she is attractive and once you marry her you need to tell her she is more than when you did before because now you are the only man in her life who can say that to her. Now she is yours and now she can concentrate on you only when it comes to her putting an effort in her looks.

If you make her feel that you don't care that today she is wearing a new dress and nice makeup then tomorrow she doesn't feel she can impress you because you don't seem to care any more. But if she sees you noticing these things when she tries for you - you end up inspiring her to get that same reaction again and again and that not just helps her keep up with her beauty quest but she will keep on getting better at it. Support her and inspire her and a woman you have married will bloom next to you every single day.

Most men suck when it comes to clothes and accessories. No woman really expects you to know anything about her wardrobe. But if you do it gives you an ultimate power over her. Suddenly she realizes that you not only do you care about the way she looks but you can make her look even more beautiful. You can actually tell her (the ultimate source of understanding what attracts the male - the male himself!) what looks good on her and what makes her look beautiful. You then suddenly become one of these precious tools (please don't take it the wrong way) of beauty she treasures so much. Why do you think we constantly ask you about how we look?

HOW DO I LOOK? DO I LOOK OK?
We are there for you to judge us, to make us feel beautiful and attractive. If you say you don't really care we will fall from the sky right back to earth and crash. We will be devastated. All this effort we put in our appearance we do it only so you will see a

beautiful woman in us. We rely on your reaction to judge if we look good or if the effort was wasted. Tell us that we look stunning, that this outfit really suits us and that you really like some detail (specify any detail in our outfit like our eye shadow or earrings and we won't take it off for days). For you these are just meaningless words but for us it's inspiration.

Every woman is an artist when it comes to her appearance and each one of us is desperate for appreciation. Give us the attention and we will get addicted to it, we will get addicted to the feeling of being admired by you. In essence we will get addicted to this sense of being with you and that, for any relationship, is a great bond to form.

#2. HER AGE

Time is our greatest enemy: we can't stop it and we can't control it and it has the full control of us and our beauty. We live each day with the knowledge that we have an expiry date (we try extremely hard to delay it of course!) and at some point we are going to be simply too old to compete with other, younger women. No matter how bad you feel every year after you have reached the "30 years on earth" mark you cannot compare it in any way to a woman who has done the same. You can argue that time is the same for everyone, men and women but it won't be true. Time truly flows differently for men.

The most important thing for a woman is her looks because that's how we attract you, men. Our brains, sense of humor and other talents can only come as additional pluses. No matter how much we want it to be different and how much we hate it that's the truth. We argue, we protest and we can burn our bras and wave our feminist equally placards until the world stands still, but in the end we know how important the way we look really is.

Alisa Miller

While we appear to be consumed by the way we look you don't have to be at all handsome for us to be attracted to you. Sure, a good looking man will get attention from us but this is never the main 'selling point' to a woman. The most important thing for a man, in our eyes, is to be strong physically as well as mentally to ensure, for us, that he can take care of us and our wellbeing. And you choose yourself what it can be - your character and ability to make us feel secure or simply being a good provider (being able to hunt a 'mammoth' for instance).

Every woman instinctively knows the structure her life has: at 20 beauty comes naturally to us, at 25 it already requires work and after 30 hard work never stops. And exactly because our youth and freshness is the main selling point for us maintaining it by fighting time is our main (but not the only one of course) priority in life.

Younger girls get excited and they want everything there and then, they want to experience every little thing because for them life runs fast and they feel that if they don't do it now they will never have a chance. So they lie about their age, make themselves look older by wearing revealing clothes and heavy makeup that generally makes girls look older than they really are. They can't wait to come of age to be able to do all the things adults do. I myself used to lie about my age when I was as young as 11. Obviously I did it online otherwise I knew that people on the other side of the screen would never take me seriously. So I lied that I was 21 in order to be accepted and talked to in chat rooms.

After 18 there is already no real need to lie about your age if you are a woman. Actually these days being 16 and hanging around guys is no longer so unusual. But as much as we try to extend the ability to freely tell our age, after 30 we still cannot do it without having second thoughts about the wisdom of having revealed it and the way it affects those who we talk in terms of how they see us.

Any modern woman would want throw something heavy at me right now for concentrating so much on age and highlighting our fear, but this is something that simply is true and no matter how hard we try to change it, it still remains a fact we have to live with.

Thanks to the advances of technology we have got better in our fight to win a piece of youth back from cruel time. This means that the length of time in which we can fearlessly announce how old we are without worrying that those who know it will lose interest in us as 'stale goods' has been extended a little.

We have got braver, as a result, and we have got prouder. We feel we should be better than that and face the facts as we grow older, concentrating on other talents to compensate for our loss in looks. But it's still every woman's personal drama and each one of us finds ways to deal with it with your help, as her man, or without it.

WHY IS SHE AFRAID TO GROW OLD?

Every woman is afraid to grow old and the explanation is quite obvious: she is either afraid that she will not be able to find a partner or she is afraid that her existing partner, who she loves, will leave her for someone younger.

So understandably growing old is a big thing for every woman. Constantly we busy ourselves in fishing for attention from you, watching carefully your reaction when we come into the room, measuring and comparing today's reaction to yesterday's, subconsciously measuring the time we have left when we effortlessly 'rule' your attention.

But we are not the only ones who suffer by this inner demon which plagues us. In order to prove to ourselves that we are safe and our future is secure we try your patience with constant questioning and testing. We watch carefully how you react to other women who are younger than us (even if it's only a couple of years difference!); those of us who are braver may ask you straight out if you are going to leave us for a younger woman eventually and watch you get out of this one. Every so often we all think about our future and we feel insecure. And this is where we exert ourselves to seek reassurance in you and your actions.

We complain. We say things we don't really mean just to see how you will react. We will point out the wrinkles we haven't seen there yet ourselves and patiently wait and see what you have got to say about them. And at the same time we are very afraid that you will actually tell us that "yes, you got older but it's a natural process of life". We hate it and we wish you could fix it for us just as well you fix everything else. Just understanding something doesn't make it easier for us to bear when it comes to something as important to us as our looks.

Some women use cosmetics to look younger and prettier and others try to avoid using anything at all hoping that by rejecting the use of chemicals they will avoid early aging. In the end we all care about the same thing. We fear you will stop being attracted to us and then we will lose any chances of keeping you by our side. That's where the headless chicken reaction takes place and suddenly playing dirty is no longer a forbidden path.

We can't control time so we control ourselves and when it fails we try to control you and your feelings and that's where things like getting pregnant/getting married come into play. Women understand that you probably won't leave them if you are bonded to them with something you can't easily leave. Like your children and your money for example so a kid(s) and a mortgage become a natural addition to every marriage. Our fear drives us through life making us sharper, we become cruel and calculating letting it to take us over until, at times, it is the only thing that controls us.

I once overheard a woman say to another, recently divorced with a kid: "See, he would never leave you if you had at least two kids 5-6 years apart from each other just so they are never old enough to understand". Shortly after that the first woman got back together with her ex-husband on a trial basis and two months later they were awaiting their second baby. As I write this they have been together for two years and now have a big mortgage and shared loans.

Fear to be left alone in the end can make us go for someone we don't really love if we feel that this person will be there for us when we lose our youth and our beauty. Sometimes fear of loneliness makes us afraid to have a relationship with anyone in the first place and we become loners of our own making just so we are able to learn how to cope with it when the time comes. Many women terrified, go into extremes, they become victims of their own fears or victimize those they love the most.

ADVICE

The age of a woman is a very sensitive subject. For most of our life it's something we hide. Simply understanding why we are so troubled with it can help you understand a lot about our motives when it comes to our behavior. If you make sure a woman you care about feels you don't see her aging she will be the happiest woman in the world. If you make her feel secure, if you can show her that she is just as attractive as ever even after 20 years of marriage. If you can never let her have the chance to doubt her looks she will adore you for that. And you on the other hand will escape years of torture and constant complaining in front of the mirror.

… # #3. HER WEIGHT

Modern women, even the brightest of us, are obsessed with our weight. There is no single modern woman on planet Earth who has never been on a diet and then discovered that with the endless options for all sort of diets you can never be off one. The standards of beauty have been developing through the centuries and since then the ideal body shape has been getting thinner and thinner so now we are facing the effect of the "disappearing woman" – a stick woman, you will barely be visible in bright daylight if she stands sideways to you.

BUT WHY ARE WE SO OBSESSED WITH IT?
It's all about control. We can't control time and aging but controlling our weight (getting slimmer = getting prettier in our minds) is something we actually can do. It doesn't mean it's easy, no, for most of us it's a lifelong, daily struggle, but we can actually do it – that is the point for us.

Not only do we put weight on faster than you, men, eating the same amount and quality of food but it's also much harder for us to then burn it all off than it is for you. And according to some of the latest studies physical exercise won't burn much fat in a woman's body even if she exercises every day while you will be able to see visible results in yourself in a very short time indeed.

Exercise helps us to shape our bodies but it does very little to burn the actual fat and this is the way nature designed us.

Being females we are designed to carry babies and at the time of pregnancy we stockpile fat for the wellbeing of our child. We are designed to store fat in our bodies so we have a better chance of surviving if it comes to carrying a baby in hard times. But there are no times which are *that* hard in the life of a modern woman any more. Giving birth is something we may do two-three times in our lifetime and weight seems to pile up each time and be harder to shift.

Going super slim is against nature but if it's what it takes to make a woman feel attractive she is prepared to pay almost any price just to get there.

We start being conscious about our body weight at a very early age. I remember myself questioning my weight when I was only 9. Seeing my mother dieting for 20 years made me feel the importance of being slim. By the age of 15 I had tried every diet available at the time. Once you get on that path there is no turning back and dieting becomes a lifestyle and a way of life.

Most women crash diet as it really is difficult to say no to a slice of bread or a piece of cake once in a while. So today she may have proper dinner with a dessert but tomorrow and probably the day after tomorrow she is going to eat only a few slices of cucumbers three times a day.

You see with age our metabolism slows down and consuming the same amount of food as we used to is no longer safe in terms of maintaining our ideal weight. The average woman puts on an extra kilogram a year if she doesn't control her diet so five years down the line she is already five kilograms heavier and that is already a big difference in her appearance. And if she eats everything she wants to she will put double or triple that in a month.

If you look at the 70s movies you see that everybody there is very slim. There were no snacks available then and no convenience foods to the degree that we have today and the snacking culture we have was not as prevalent. People still prepared meals from scratch. Nowadays snacking is something everybody does all the time missing the fact that it is still food and has a calorie value (and a high calorie value at that!). A small pack of nuts for example contains about 900 kcal each which is almost half of the daily calorie intake for the average woman. How are you supposed to burn it off? Running 5km on a treadmill will not burn even half of that.

Traps like that surround women every day: a pack of nuts on the way to work, a sandwich at lunch, maybe a chocolate bar for dessert and then a full meal in the evening. But a modern woman can't afford that if she wants you to be attracted to her. IF. 'If' is a good word.

WHY DOES SHE PUT WEIGHT ON?

There are so many reasons which answer this question I really do not know where to start from.

Food is the shortest and easiest way to make someone feel good. It's like a drug for most people. We feel good after a good meal, we feel even better after the dessert after the meal and this feeling gets imprinted in our minds. If you feel low or you feel sad you try to find a way to make yourself feel better. Different people have different ways of dealing with it but when it comes to women who are already suffering on crash diets it becomes *the* way to feel better instantly (till the beach season comes and you suddenly realize you are not a bikini kind of babe any more).

Women don't just eat to feel better but they seriously overeat because they know they are going to crash diet after that (or they think they will). They are trying to make the good feeling last by consuming as much food as they can fit in. A lot of them eventually get depressed because suddenly they are cut off from this good feeling of fullness. All they can think of at that point is food and they get locked in a cycle of food binges and deprivation which seriously affects their state of mind.

When they eat they feel good but once it's over they feel guilty and they promise they are going to crash diet starting from tomorrow. But tomorrow they feel sad because now they have to diet and break the promise to cheer themselves up once again. It never stops really unless a woman makes herself stop or someone else does it for her. And the more she eats the better she feels, the stronger the imprint in her mind becomes. And at some point it becomes the dominant feeling of joy she can have in her life and everything else stops giving her pleasure. When eventually she gets fat and she can no longer ignore it she has to go on a diet for real and the torture of it is probably like what drug addicts have to go through when they are trying to get clean and have to undergo through a period of severe withdrawal symptoms.

Unfortunately the promise of pleasure and joy is too attractive and food, well, is much easier to get hold of than drugs.

BURNING IT OFF

As I said earlier exercise does help but it doesn't help much when it comes to burning fat off in a woman's body. We are designed to store fat and this is exactly what our body does and, unfortunately, it does it very well indeed.

When we crash diet we make our body go into shock and start using up the fat it has stored up for a rainy day. The longer we stay on a diet the more fat our body will be willing to use up in order to survive. But our body is clever, it has its own logic system. If it's used to dieting it knows that eventually it's going to get food and there is no real need to burn anything at all so in the first stages of a diet a woman will undergo terrible torture as her body will not get rid of any fat at all and she will have no energy to make her go through the day and then only after a few days when there will be no more resources to use up will her body give in and start burning up its stored reserves of fat.

So what happens if a woman gets off the diet and has a proper meal straight after that? Every woman's horror is what happens. Her body, starved for resources (food), starts storing every little bit leaving very little to go to waste. And instead of getting thinner or even maintaining the weight she dropped to she gets fatter. And this is why a lot of dieticians advise women to stick to lifestyle dieting and train their bodies to expect being fed the same amounts every time.

Alisa Miller

#4. HER AND OTHER WOMEN

When it comes to explaining about the 'sisterhood' to men I always use the three women in the room scenario because it shows best the way women relate to each other.

You would think that women, just like men, get on with each other well but it doesn't quite work that way. Three women in a room alone will be on friendly terms, sure thing. There will be girl talk, some bonding which comes because of the shared sex and much social talk.

Once it's a room with three women and a guy, however, they suddenly become competitors. And that's where any notion of sisterhood stops. Here is the interesting fact few men can grasp: Although all three women will try and fight for the man's attention, provided all of them are interested in him, it doesn't necessarily mean all three really want him.

It doesn't matter if any of them are married or have boyfriends they will all try and prove that they can "beat" one another. It's pretty much like this: as important as it is for you to win a girl's attention it is the same for women when it comes to men.

The only exception from the rule is a girl who is already passionate about someone else to the point that she really cannot be bothered to seek affirmation of her attractiveness by playing this game. But even she may try to get this guy's attention just to prove to herself that she can. The difference between her and other girls is that she won't try as hard as they will.

Every time we get some attention in any occasion we feed our ego. It helps us feel better about ourselves and it makes us more confident. You may think here what's in it for you as our guy? Quite a lot actually. Imagine a flower in a pot. If it's not being looked after it may grow but it won't be as pretty as if you had fed it and taken good care of it. Every flower needs watering, feeding and looking after. And did you know that flowers actually grow better and have a better bloom if you talk to them or leave them near classical music? It all takes effort. And it is the same with women. We need compliments, we need attention, we need to feed our ego in order to be beautiful.

If we feel that no one is watching and no one cares about how we look, we don't get enough competition or we feel there is nothing to fight for we stop trying and give up on ourselves and that can have devastating consequences where a woman's looks and sense of identity are concerned.

Alisa Miller

So if your girlfriend or your wife stopped caring about the way she looks there is an easy way to fix it. Actually two. First, tell her how beautiful she is and how bright her eyes sparkle long enough for her to start trying to fish it out from you again and again. Second, let her stay in a room with two gorgeous women at a party or any other celebration. It will immediately set her competitive ego to work. She will envy their looks and the effect it has on other men and start re-evaluating her own.

In general, women don't have many women friends. Most of us form small groups and call them best friends or "circles of trust". But it's not the same as the friendship men can have. Once a guy comes into a circle like that it stops being anything associated with trust and begins to look like a battle ring for female egos.

Mothers, daughters, sisters, best friends we are all driven by the same hungry ego. We need to feel wanted, we need to feel attractive and we need to feel that we, at any moment, can find any mate we want.

This constant drive for attention and competitiveness helps explain something else men rarely understand: A pretty girl with an ugly friend is something you will get as a given – we don't like constant competition.

So if you ask your friend's pretty girlfriend to match you up with her friend expecting that her friends will be as gorgeous as she is, you may well end up having a long evening with a female version of Quasimodo. Not necessarily, of course, but it is quite likely. Pretty girls don't like having competition by their side all the time and having someone not so good looking makes them look better on that front anyway.

Beautiful girls hate each other. They don't get along. They need somebody much less beautiful than themselves to feel good about the way they look. Also if they constantly win the battle of "Three women in a room" with a friend like that, it feeds their ego when the guy (obviously) goes for them but not their ugly friend.

So how does the 'ugly' friend benefit then? Well, first of all next to a pretty friend they will also look better in the eyes of a guy, it's just the way it works. And second, there may be more then just one guy in a room and he most likely will go for her if the pretty one is already taken by his own friend. Maybe not for the looks but looks is not all that counts when it comes to getting with a girl.

One guy gets a hot girl then his friend has to pick up whoever is left (but this may be a better deal as she might be more fun or simply better in bed). Less pretty girls just have to try harder to find a guy. And most likely you'll see them in the company of gorgeous beauty queens.

There is no sisterhood when it comes to women. There is only a truce. We still need friends through but there are a lot of 'buts' in this relationship. Women will always relate to each other as an enemy if it comes to a guy they are both interested in.

SO WHAT DO WE UNDERSTAND BY 'COMPETITION'?

Well, Angelina Jolie for example is no competition unless we end up with her and a guy we like in one room. Of cause this would be an unfair battle as a lot of girls wouldn't mind sleeping with her never mind guys, but this doesn't mean we won't try to get the guy, either.

We know we will lose but we won't lose face and if we win in that kind of situation, our ego will be fed and happy for many years to come.

So who is competition? Our "friends" mostly and women we have constant contact with. And the more contact with better looking women we have the harder we are going to work on our own beauty and style. If we don't 'get' the challenge which comes from a better looking woman in a room we stop trying hard to impress anybody as we don't feel there is a need to try hard any more. A woman needs to feel attractive or she 'loses it' and starts to turn into a pumpkin.

WHEN WE DON'T TAKE OTHER WOMEN SERIOUSLY AS COMPETITION

We don't think a woman is competition for us when she is much older or much younger (like a girl who hasn't even reached puberty) then she is OK.

A woman who doesn't have any contact with us like a movie star who can only be seen on screen is not competition, neither is a woman we know will never cross into real life for us at any time is considered competition.

A woman who is extremely ugly, a woman missing vital body parts, a woman who has poor hygiene are also considered to be no competition. Hopefully you begin to understand. Everybody else is competition.

Younger girls seem to look up to older women because they want to copy them. And older women often encourage younger women to get the man they want as a sport (providing there is a significant difference in age or they have no common interest in a guy).

The same rule applies to anything another woman may want. A piece of furniture or a fashion item we want will make us tear each other apart for it (one reason you should avoid going to sales with your girlfriend or a wife – an unwelcome transformation really does take place).

But if you are in a circle of trust and it's not about a guy we will let things slide. The thing about being a woman however is that we know that at any time and at any given moment the truce can be broken and all-out war may indeed break out.

Alisa Miller

#5. WHY SHE HATES YOUR MOTHER

The question of why the woman in your life does not get on with your mother is one that's often asked and rarely answered. So let's take this one from the beginning. First, it's not actually your mother she hates, but that other woman in your life. Asking your girlfriend or your wife to love your mother is just like asking her to have a threesome with some girl you just met down the pub. You have to be gentle about it and have your strategy all worked out if you want to have a positive outcome.

See, between women no matter what age or skin colour or sexual preferences it's all about attention. We know that no matter how hard we try your mother will always be your mother and command the centre of your attention and that is exactly why we are so pissed off about it.

We'll make the face, we'll play the role but we'll never really truly see her the way you do. Just as she will never accept that her beloved son chose the 'monster' which is us and ignored the millions of "nice girls" he could have had instead which she would (possibly) found more acceptable to her.

I know it gets confusing but it's all about the old game about who 'owns' you once we are in one room with you. And that's why you need to be extremely clever about it to keep both sides happy. You see, the only reason we hate her (or rather don't like her much) is because we feel we have to know who is more important to you: us or her. No matter how ridiculous it may sound we fight with her for the number one spot in your heart.

In order to escape that kind of situation you need to manipulate both sides of the (probable) conflict. So for your own good make sure your girlfriend/wife knows that you don't care what your mum thinks of her (even if you do). That way you'll instantly save yourself a lot of trouble in having to prove this to her later (and she will ask for proof repeatedly) and she'll feel that she has won before the battle has even began.

See, the truth is every woman is worried as hell when she meets her partner's mother and when (if) things go wrong and she senses that his mother is against her then she has no other choice but to fight back.

Normally for that she'll use you. If we think that your mother doesn't like us we are afraid that she will try and make you see us differently, have doubts about us and even leave us. So our first reaction is to check if you are on our side and that's when we carefully try and make negative remarks about your mum. It doesn't mean we are bitchy. We are scared to death. We are trying to see if you care about us more then you care about what your mother has to say about us.

All the hate actually comes from insecurity and the fear of another woman who we know. We understand that she gave you life and is the closest woman to you apart from us, who has powers over you and your feelings.

On the other hand your mother will probably hate us for the very same reason. She is afraid that someone else is going to take her 'boy' away and she will no longer be the only one in his life.

ADVICE

If you play it smart and if you can manage both sides you'll (hopefully) never know what's it like to be in the middle of the deadly battle between the two women you care about, your partner and your mother.

Let each one of us know that there is nothing to be afraid of. Make sure you give your mum more attention when you find a girlfriend (aka us) or get married so she doesn't feel that that new woman in her son's life is stealing her son's attention away from her.

On the other hand let your beloved know that no matter how your mother feels about her it will never change your feelings towards her.

Look out for negative remarks and agree with them for your own good but then make sure you always add: "Yes, you are right, but she is my mother I can't do anything about that". You think that we are just going to push you from this point on? We also understand the relationship you have with her. We just get emotional and need to be reminded of it from time to time.

Well, actually once we establish that your mother is no threat to us we will start to like her. We will encourage you to visit her and even may become good friends with her. Well, you already know what 'good friends' means when it comes to relationships between women. It may not be a completely smooth, easy-going friendship but we'll make the effort so it will be as close to friendship as we can make it.

You need to understand that it's all about wining you all over again. We don't really hate your mother; we fear her or rather, we fear the power we imagine she has over you. Illuminate that fear and make it go away and you'll never have a problem like that in your life with us again.

Alisa Miller

#6.
COMPLIMENTING OTHER WOMEN

This is a subject which many a woman has unloaded to me, in my professional capacity, as a source of issues with her partner so let's get right down to it.

Unless you are suicidal you never compliment other women when the woman you care about is present. By saying that someone else, not her, has a nice voice, nice legs, nice anything at all is like saying that you are into that woman and you actually like her. Even if she is ugly and old but you found something nice to say about her it immediately sets us off.

Remember that we, women, don't really like each other that much because we constantly compete for your attention. So something that seems like an innocent remark to you can make us feel very angry towards the other woman. Remember that a positive remark made about the good looks of our friend can make us 'forget' that friend's phone number for months.

Maintaining our looks is a full time job and when you notice how good other women look it makes us feel that we have failed. We hate it when you do that but we won't tell you openly about it. We will keep quite about it but we will make you feel that something is wrong. If you sense that something is wrong and ask we will say it's 'nothing'. This is one of these 'nothings' that annoy the hell out of you because you sense that there is actually 'something' and we will not talk about it.

You see, you're right, we can't justify openly why we got frustrated with you so we try and find something else we can object to in your actions. But all we are really concerned about at that point is you reacting to the other woman who took your attention (for a millisecond or two?) away from us.

It doesn't really matter what exactly you found nice about her we objected to. And depending on how important it is to us (the hair, the legs, the ass, the color of her eyes) the deeper will be the effect it has on us. Especially if it is something we can't control about ourselves or we are failing to achieve at the moment (like being slim and looking good in that kind of dress).

It's like telling us that someone is better and not just someone we don't know and whom you and we will never meet, but someone within your reach. We don't object so much if you comment on an actress or a singer because we know they are out there somewhere and pretty unreachable. But if the woman you complimented is in the same room with us then it becomes a whole new ball game because this is where we are competitors and right now she is winning. And there is more in there for us because you are already our man and it becomes a question of someone else hunting in our territory. We get pissed off. We make faces. We hide the way we feel or we tell you straight how we feel and then you will have to find a way to prove to us that we are the best and that it wasn't a meaningful remark at all.

ADVICE
If you just said something nice about another woman and you need to save yourself from our anger you need to give us something satisfying enough to calm down our ego. The "ass" comment works 99% of the time. Even if the girl has a perfect ass just tell us that it's either too skinny or too big. We will want to believe you so much that we will no matter how big of a lie it is, we will calm down immediately. Otherwise just keep it to yourself if you liked something about another woman unless you are going to add straight after that: "But your (insert the asset here) is so much better!"

#7. WHAT HAPPENS WHEN YOU NOTICE OTHER WOMEN

Looking doesn't hurt anybody – or, at least, so they say. And when you look at other women this is exactly how you justify it. After all this is part of being a man - being aware of good looking women around you. Unfortunately this is not the way we see it. Being a stud is something you can joke about amongst your friends but paying attention to other women when we are around works like a red rag in front of a bull. We will not just hate you for that but we will make sure you suffer for every millisecond of this "just looking".

We women are very territorial when it comes to our men. And even if we don't feel much towards our present partner we will rush to the defense of our property like a wired farmer with a shotgun. And it's not really about us thinking that you may actually do anything beyond looking or you actually feel attracted to someone else (logically that would be the answer) but the true reason of us getting so pissed off is because by looking you are admitting that someone else is better looking than we are.

A woman caught in this kind of situation will tear you to pieces (metaphorically speaking) but in fact it's not you she has in mind at that point. In reality she is frustrated with herself and her inability to match that other woman you have just given a high 'score' to. She won't actually admit that to you or to herself and, in all likelihood, she will end up taking her frustration out on you.

ADVICE

Handling a frustrated woman is not an easy task that's why understanding why she is frustrated is vital. There is too much risk that you will say the wrong thing and, based on what you know and others say, tackle it incorrectly which will then make things escalate.

The wrong response to avoid: Once you end up with "looking and being caught" your first reaction is to let her know that it meant nothing. I understand it is instinctive and probably true, but here's the thing: it never works!

It never works immediately and it barely lets you survive her fury. Why? Because this is a pointless thing to say never mind the fact that it's a used up cliché. If you think that her main concern is you being faithful at that point you are wrong. At that point all she can think of is herself and her looks and the fact that she just lost to another woman. And not just losing in the attention stakes from other men but losing the attention of HER man. Of course she is pissed off. Right now in her head you are more likely to find thoughts like: "F*cking moron she wasn't even that good! Shit what am I going to do? Should I change something about myself? He is already looking at other women, am I getting old? Maybe it's my hair?" And after that she may think about the future of your relationship and you staying faithful to her. Maybe.

So you see it actually means a lot more to her than it does to you and it affects her much more deeply than you thought.

CORRECT RESPONSES TO REMEMBER
Forget the excuses and clichés. All she needs right know is for you to attack that 'other' woman and reinstate your partner as your number one (and only one) desirable woman, beauty standard and object of affection and attention in your life. You need to convince her she is so good the rest of the world will never be able to match her looks.

How do you do that?

It's quite simple actually. All you have to do is find an excuse for you looking at the 'other' woman which is totally opposite to the real one.

You didn't look at that hottie because she was actually hot but because you have never seen such a weird way of walking. Yeah, ridiculous you think? But it works. She will eat it up like a piece of the finest tart. No matter what you say, what is important is that you give a score back to your woman and discredit the one you were just admiringly looking at.

To help you out here a little here are some lines which I have noticed boyfriends or husbands of some of my friends use quite successfully:

"She had a piece of toilet paper stuck on her shoe."

"I was just trying to see if it was a wig she was wearing, she looked funny."

"She smelled a little when she passed by." (Try to look disgusted.)

"I heard a rumour about her being a slut, that 10 guys did her in the office." (Try to look disgusted.)

"There was gum in her hair." (Look disgusted.)

"She has a huge ass for such a little girl." (When the ass of your partner is absolutely perfect!)

"I saw that girl at the dentist and heard her calling her boyfriend and telling him that she has an STD."

"I am pretty sure that's the girl guys at work were laughing at the other day because she is so ****** stupid."

The point here is that you need to be creative but be careful of what you say. And you know how you need to look when you say it. Don't discredit yourself trying to discredit her and be realistic about your lying talents. If you do it right you will successfully escape a huge long-lasting argument.

"Poor thing!", - you will hear her saying, victoriously.

#8. THE DEAL WITH YOUR EX

Women are extremely territorial creatures even if they seem not to be. This is especially true when it comes to your ex. Because we understand how deeply we affect you and how difficult it becomes to forget it all after we are gone we know it is important to make sure that the territory (aka you) is cleared (all the evil spirits have been exorcised) and reclaimed. Depending on how long you have been with your ex the harder we will try to erase her from your memory and we are constantly being haunted by her ghost.

If you want to get yourself a nightmare girlfriend tell her about your perfect ex. What you had with another woman before you should always leave behind or at least you should never discuss your previous life (especially if there is something good to remember) with your current girlfriend or any woman you've just met and think you like.

Alisa Miller

It's very simple: if you are still in love with your ex you don't start a new relationship, it will have no future unless you've made a clean break with the past. This means that when it comes to your current relationship, anything you say regarding your ex has to be either negative or otherwise be kept to yourself.

Although we are always dying to find out every little bit about your previous relationship you should never tell us anything about it. You see, we understand that at some point you felt something for that person and deeply inside we are afraid that you still do no matter how long ago it happened between you. If you tell us that your ex was a good cook we will die inside and try and learn to be just as good as she was, if not better. But it won't make us happy; it will make us miserable because it won't be something we will enjoy, it'll be a small personal torture imposed by our own selves. In the end we will blame you if we fail. We will try and compete with a ghost, trying to prove to you that we are just as good, trying to get you to say that we are actually much better than she had ever been. And this is exactly what it is going to be all about if we ever get hold of any positive information about your ex.

It's very difficult for a woman to accept that you've already done something before with a woman you used to be in love with and you enjoyed it in the past. Then we will feel that with us it's nothing more but a repetition and not a new and exciting experience. That's why you must never take us to the same places you used to go with your ex and you must never ask us to learn something your ex used to do well or at least never let us know it's something she used to do or you used to do with her. It will kill us if we think even for a second that we are just a replacement. And competing with your perfect past which can never fail (because it has already happened and it's in the past) can be very destructive for any woman.

If you are still in contact with your ex for whatever reason the first thing you must do is convince us (again and again) that she doesn't mean anything to you anymore and even if you have to lie you have to tell us that she is nothing compared to us.

This is just something you either tell us or we will squeeze it out from you ourselves through constant nagging and questioning designed to help us get some positive affirmation about ourselves.

So save us and yourself time and energy and get it over with. We will never stand competition and we will fight hard to keep you away from your past using all sort of ways both moral and questionable, including contacting her and spelling things out ourselves. If you think that two friends can have a fight over a guy they both like then imagine how two women who had the same guy (had sex with him and all the other romantic and passionate moments) would deal with each other. It's a massacre.

This is something we are not able to control: the way we feel about a woman who had you and a woman you felt tender for before us. We can't stand the thought that you could have been happy before you met us. We always believe that when we met you it was the whole new beginning and a new start for both of us and leaving a place in your life for your ex would only mean that you still care about someone else but us.

You see we women believe in ownership. We let you own us but we expect you to give yourself to us in return. And not 50% of you, or 80% or 99.9% but the full 100% of your love, care and attention. There is no such thing as loving two women at the same time. You can like a thousand women but you can love just one. Everything else is a compromise and basically a lie where you don't have to make a choice between them.

You can care about your ex, but you can't care about her more than you care about your current partner, that would be wrong and she will be right to be mad about it and even leave you as a result. You need to understand how deeply it affects us when you still care about your ex and that it really hurts when you say good things about her. Even if she is a good woman she is no longer your woman and everything positive you say about her to your current partner will only destroy your current relationship. Don't ask us to understand why you care because we will lie and pretend we do to please you but inside we will constantly be in pain every time you mention her name.

ADVICE
You never keep any cards of your ex or photographs of your ex in the house or anywhere your current girlfriend or new wife can find them. You never say anything good about your ex or compare her aloud to your current partner, unless you really want your current relationship to be over very soon. You don't keep in touch or if you do make sure your current partner knows about it (and you tell her again and again) that you absolutely hate these contacts.

We will never be 100% calm about your ex unless you make us believe that time with her was a living hell and you hated every second of it. And even if you are lying when you say it, it's better than having a paranoid partner on your hands.

BEING THE 'OTHER' WOMAN

Here you need to think carefully about what I am going to say because it will help you understand why so many men think women give them the 'wrong' signals or misunderstand them when they, have made it clear from the start, that they are not interested in anything more than a fling or a little harmless flirting or maybe a little casual sex.

As women we always fight, so to speak, for pretty much everything: the best spot under the sun, the last handbag on sale, you, men, no matter who you belong to at the time. And when it comes to flirting with someone who is taken we don't see it as a big deal; after all the guy is responding to us and that means that whatever he has (or rather whoever he has) in his love life is not that important to him. So when a man says to a woman that he is (happily) married or has a girlfriend all it means to us is that he can perform sexually on a daily basis and very rarely does it mean that there might be a "problem" in moving forward with a new relationship.

When we think about a man having an 'official' partner (as in a wife or a long-term partner) and us becoming the 'other' woman we actually don't think about it. Our brain suddenly cuts out all the details of your 'other' life and we completely ignore the fact itself. We don't imagine you leaving us and going back to someone else and having a good time. What we imagine is you being trapped in an unwanted relationship and suffering every second you are away from us in the arms of that monster – your wife, or girlfriend.

We certainly don't think that your wife or your girlfriend is someone you love otherwise why would you spend time talking to us? You must be unhappy. And just on the basis of that we feel that it's OK to become "the other woman". Of course, it's not like we ever think that this situation is going to last forever, we hope that at some point we are going to become *The One* once you 'deal' with your situation.

It's true that in most cases this is a naïve expectation. Whether it is sheer wishful thinking or a defense mechanism which allows the female brain to rationalize a situation so it can be dealt with is debatable. The truth is however that this is how most women operate when it comes to becoming 'the other woman' and it allows them to become attached to unavailable men, it also allows unavailable men to get mistresses, so everyone's happy on this score, which might suggest an underlying biological imperative. Until, however, we have a number of studies on this and some hard data, this remains firmly in the realm of the hypothetical which leaves us only the facts that affairs and trysts do happen and they happen far more frequently and with greater ease than a committed relationship between two people should allow.

HOW THE 'OTHER' WOMAN'S BRAIN WORKS

This is how 'the other woman's' brain works. She thinks (and in most cases truly believes) that it's her you really want by your side, even if you made it crystal clear that you are not going to leave your partner for her.

She will, in her own mind, expect you to actually leave your current partner and situation and, at some point, she will probably even try and push you to do exactly that.

You see, there is no joy knowing that you share your bed with someone else and worse than that, that that person actually has more rights to do so and doesn't need to hide it from the rest of the world. That's why 'the other woman' prefers to ignore the very fact of being the other woman and, if she really likes you that much, will go along with the most extreme (and sometimes bizarre) set of circumstances in the hope (and unacknowledged expectation) that things will change.

There is a simplicity to this argument which is used as justification that is almost brilliant: why would you be there with her instead of your partner? Why would you flirt? Why would you spend time with someone else if you are happy in your existing relationship? It's very easy to misunderstand you and twist your words. It's not like we will ever accept that you might be just a little bored with your safe, predictable life and want to get some excitement (and some sex) on the side.

'The other woman' takes the view that if you are flirting with her and want to take it further you are not happy in your current relationship. She takes the view that this situation of her being the other woman is temporary and that at some point it's going to change and she will become the only woman in your life.

Odd as this may sound it is the way the female mind, predominantly, works. This often leads (as you can guess) to a deep misunderstanding in expectations between the sexes. At this point, with everything we have covered, you begin to see, I hope, just why there are so many hopeless relationships

Alisa Miller

and so many affairs start with the only possible ending being misery and pain.

#9. YOU: THE MAN SHE IS LOOKING FOR

Before turning to writing full time I used to give lectures on relationships and why they go wrong. I used to say (and this is not an original joke) that every man wants his woman to be good in bed, good with his friends and a good cook. That's why he normally ends up with three women.

When a woman is looking for her perfect man the list of requests is endless. And yet there are three things in a man that can satisfy her 100%.

When a woman is looking for a perfect man she wants him first of all to be a man – strong, reliable, and a good provider. And when I say strong it has nothing to do with physical strength. Although being physically strong also can help to win her heart it can never give a woman the same satisfaction that the emotional strength of her partner will give her.

Alisa Miller

Women hate men who can't make decisions, who can't take action when action is required, and who can't shield them. And as a result women take the burden on their shoulders. Women in such relationships seize the initiative and become manlier and they hate it. We feel that if you don't do what must be done we have to!

If we are stuck in a relationship with a guy who can't make a move without our approval, can't look after us and protect us from the outside world we absolutely hate that guy and make his (as well as our own) life unbearable. We take the strong side and we lead the family (or the relationship) hating every second of it because we are under stress.

So in order for us to be feminine and sensitive, to take time (and pleasure) in being women, we need a man who we can trust to take care of us, protect and guard our vulnerability. That kind of man is really difficult to find these days. Yet we never lose hope that we will find one.

When we are looking for a perfect man we are also looking for a good lover. Despite what most spam emails you receive will have you believe, being a good lover has nothing to do with size and it even has little to do with experience. Your knowledge of every page of the Kama Sutra won't make any difference to us if you don't know what you are doing once you get there. And what's more important if you don't ask and don't listen.

A few years ago I took a poll of women I knew (and who I trusted to answer truthfully) to find out how many of them actually orgasmed during sex with their partners. I hope you are sitting down right now. The poll showed that not one of them was happy with their sex life with their partners. And some of them were in long term relationships and purported to be happy in them. Each one of the women I asked had never experienced an orgasm with their partner.

So what, you may ask, didn't their partners notice? Well, the thing is unless we tell you you'll never know. Faking an orgasm is something we can do as easily as blinking. We always know what you expect to see and hear and we do just the thing. It's easier for us to be done with it so we can move on to other things. We know you need it and we provide it but it doesn't mean we enjoy it; it's more of a duty to us. If we don't feel secure with you and if we feel you don't care then when having sex with you we feel absolutely nothing. We could just as well read a book in the process.

So how can you be a good lover? It's simple. You don't need to be experienced, you don't need to be physically gifted, you just need to ask us and listen to what we've got to say. But don't just ask what we like in the sort of coy, half-hearted way you might ask us whether we want a cappuccino or a latte. You have to ask directly and make the questions part of your time with us. Don't, for example, ask: "What do you like". Instead ask "Do you like it when I do this?", "When do you like it?". Female sexuality is a multiphasic thing. The way we respond in bed starts with the way we feel about how we look, in our head. There is a good chance that many women will not feel very comfortable enough to answer straight away so you have to be patient, but never leave questions unanswered if you want your relationship to work.

Most of us will try to please you 99% of the time so unless you dig to get to the truth you will never find it. A man who perseveres, who experiments with his partner, who makes his partner's body not just an instrument of pleasure for himself but a mutual area to be explored and savored and mutually enjoyed, is a man who shows that he is investing time, effort and emotion in bonding with his partner. That man, a woman knows, is well worth trying hard to keep.

Finally, the last but not the least of the three requirements is that when we are looking for a perfect man we are looking for a friend. As I told you before a friendship between two women is a funny thing and can be just as easily broken when facing difficulties (or when a potentially available male is nearby). In most cases the friendship between two women is a union, with a truce and it works only as long as the two women don't have competing interests. And yet we always need someone we can trust.

If you turn out to be the kind of man we can trust you with all our secrets then you are the perfect man we've been looking for. But we need to feel we can trust you. Getting someone's trust to that extent is never an instant thing (and you should immediately be suspicious of it, if it happens immediately). It takes time and once again patience. We all know that it makes us vulnerable to open up to someone we know who then will judge us. And that's what we are so afraid of, your judgment. Make us feel that no matter what we say you'll always understand, support us and be on our side. Tell us that, keep telling us that, and never stop telling us that and you're onto a winner.

When we are looking for a perfect man we are looking for that special person we will be able to share the whole world with, big and small things equally. A lot of women would even fall for their best friends just because they feel that closeness they can't find in anybody else (which is why women are so ready to have lesbian relationships). We are always looking for a man who will complete us mentally as well as physically.

We are all looking for a protector and a guardian, for a lover and a best friend. And once we find one (if we get that lucky) we will never need anybody else because we have already found the man we were looking for all our lives.

WHY GOOD GIRLS LIKE BAD GUYS

I know that many a man has spent many a sleepless night wondering just what he has to do to get a date. He may be decent, polite, clean, maybe even a high earner with a good career and prospects and yet he may be finding that women are not willing to go out with him very easily and once they do it rarely leads to anything serious or long-lasting.

These are the same guys who know that their James Dean-type, devil-may-care counterparts are finding it difficult to fit in all the women in their life.

Here's a truth: Men score in numbers when women score in quality. For a woman to capture a bad guy is a high score even if she is not planning to spend the rest of her life with this particular individual. She will still want to try to see if her power (as a woman) works on him.

In most cases she finds it hard going, particularly if the person she is interested in is a real 'bad guy' (he will then probably pay no attention to her tricks). So now she is the one who is being played here and that deserves some admiration.

Every woman will try it on with the bad guy just to prove to herself she can have him. If she can't, well, she will die trying. And you know what every woman thinks? That it will be different with her and that she will change him. She'll be the one who 'marks' him and makes him abandon the ways which make him so attractive to her, at the time, and agree to become, for her, a settled, career person.

Good girls like bad guys because they excite them with a whole new world they have never experienced before (otherwise they would not be so "good" would they?).

What has he got to offer to her? Excitement. You see, love and care she can find almost everywhere else but excitement and the feeling of being on edge is something she just wants to experience at least once in her lifetime.

I know you'd think that a 'sensible' analysis would tell her he is the wrong guy for her. Unfortunately, two things conspire against that. The first is that the sense of excitement is heady and addictive. She likes it, she thinks the world looks and feels better through it. The second is that somewhere deep inside she dreams she can change him. Eventually excitement and overflowing emotions pass and all she is left with is a man without a future. Unless he dumps her first.

Yet there will always be a good girl who will be fascinated by the whole new world a 'bad' guy has to offer. If you are one of these bad guys you will probably find it very easy to score. But there is a drawback in all this because any relationship you have either doesn't last long when you want it to or it does and you wish you could get rid of the girl you have.

We, humans, are programmed to try and taste the forbidden fruit. Yeah, you know how it goes: the more she feels that she shouldn't be with the guy she's with the more she wants him. Anybody she finds easy to get doesn't interest her; what she really wants is the guy she can't have. Just like you would want the girl every other guy wants and can't get.

Alisa Miller

#10. THE SEDUCTION RITUAL & FLIRTING

Just as much as you need porn, beer and hot women magazines we, women, need flirting. Each one of us needs to feel wanted and needed and unfortunately, most of us need more affection and attention from the opposite sex than one man can possibly give us. Every woman needs to feel that at any given moment she can have a man of her choosing if she really wants to. It's not a particular task we set out to accomplish or a thing we feel compelled to prove, but it makes us feel good to think we can do it and it's a challenge where scoring points is going to feed our ego for weeks (or even months) ahead.

Men find this difficult to understand. It comes from the deep sense of insecurity most of us have but it is also part of our biological programming as women - we have to make sure that our future is secure and we can still hunt a man down if we are in need of one.

When a woman flirts with you she doesn't necessarily want you, I would say, most probably she doesn't because we all flirt from time to time just to feel good about ourselves. Here is an area where the two sexes approach each other with huge, preconceived notions which often can lead to trouble: Feeling being wanted and being had are two very different things. Flirting, for a woman, never actually implies sex. You, men, tend to always attach one to the other, when for her it's always a game and a game only.

There is no difference between flirting and flirting with intention for a woman. If she wants something from you, she will take it to the next level herself and will let you know if she is available. Being aggressive in a situation with a flirting woman is the worst thing you could possibly do. When she flirts all she wants to do is to find out if you like her and it may be the main goal of the whole thing (most of the time anyway) but if she is really interested in you she will definitely give you a chance to move forward with it.

Here's where it often gets confusing: if she reacts positively to you and flirts back it doesn't mean she actually wants to move forward, it's part of the 'feel-good' game she's engaged in. If, however.

she is willing to stay with you longer or meet with you again then there may be something else on her mind besides just scoring a point or two to feed her ego.

We, women, get excited by the idea that we can have anyone and the men who are harder to get excite us the most. Especially when there is another woman (or women) involved. We like men who are surrounded by other women and even, well, when they are married because it's a challenge for us. Besides at a deeper, primal level, seeing a married man, to us, is like seeing an already proven good product (lots of women are dying to be with that man – he must be good). Certified.

Apart from the hunt for attention in order to feel wanted we also get bored and flirting is one of these socially acceptable games which we feel we can play without causing any harm. In our minds we don't actually realize we give you false hope, we simply see it as both of us having a good time without anyone getting hurt.

When it comes to seduction again getting you and then having you are not necessarily two things which for us are connected. This is where, most often, the 'wrong signals' are definitely given with men and women often getting mixed up in their heads in terms of what they want and what it is that they are getting into. As women, we feel that if we don't get your attention by flirting it doesn't mean we are just going to move on to the next subject, we just need to try a little harder.

You see, we feel that the goal (i.e. to get your attention) is well within our reach (otherwise we wouldn't have tried and, at that stage, we are not going to believe it's not because it's a blow to our ego which is what has led us to this course of action in the first place). So, the harder the goal the harder we will probably try to get your response. But then, when we have you it doesn't mean we are planning to keep you. Sometimes we are just cruel monsters and the worst of it is we can't help it! To us it's a game and it is all OK!

It drives us, this need to be liked and wanted, pretty much through our whole life. We want to look good, we want to be attractive and we want to be able to get any man any time. Yet, it is still all a game and in the end all we want is just the one guy we feel we can love. Flirting is a hunt, it's a tease and it gives us pleasure but it doesn't lead to much of anything (for us) most of the time. Unless, of course, we flirt for sex and we want to be used – then it's your lucky night.

ADVICE
How do you handle this disparity in approach as a guy without running the risk of misreading the signals, going too far and coming across like some Neanderthal fresh out of the caves?

Go with the flow, react but be polite. If she is interested in you she will respond but being aggressive and pushing when a woman flirts with you is not a good idea. Flirt back lightly and see where it's going to take you. Probably nowhere two times out of three but there is still a chance that she is going to take it further that one time out of three.

After all, women also have needs. There is an undeniable power in being able to lose yourself in sex. In case you are in a steady relationship and are worried reading this, relax. We all need a soul mate in the end and although the game never stops, the hunt does. A woman is capable of being totally faithful, no matter what temptation she faces, if she really loves her man and is committed to him. Sex, for her, never 'just happens'.

WHY DOES SHE WANT TO CHANGE YOU?

Here is a familiar scenario: When you just started dating she seemed to love you just the way you were. But with time you noticed that once in a while she'd try to tell you how to behave or what to wear. If you are in this situation then it seems that suddenly the girl who adored you for yourself now wants you to be someone else.

Well, all women try to make their man better. It's our nature to want more from you than you immediately give us and then more and more after that. After the excitement of the first dates is gone we begin to see all the little faults we hadn't noticed before and depending on how bearable these faults are we will rush to fix them.

It's not that she doesn't accept you for who you are, she does, but she doesn't want to accept that you can't change for her either. A lot of women date men they don't think are good for their future but they are in love with and they hope that eventually these men will change for them.

We all know how that tends to work out. The thing is that unfortunately women don't just believe that the change in their man is a possibility - some of us are absolutely convinced that you will change for us.

For example, if you tell her that you will never throw something away because you love it, or you won't move to another town because your friends are all here or that you will never change your job, listening to all that, a woman nods and thinks: "We shall see".

It's not that she doesn't love you but unfortunately she doesn't like some of your habits. It's very difficult to meet someone who is your perfect fit and everything about that person is perfect for you. So when a woman meets a near-perfect man she is too afraid to lose him and simply plans to change him later on into the man she really dreamed of.

It's quite ironic but all you want from us is not to change after marriage and all we want from you is to change completely. But it's something we will never tell you or even talk about and we'll try and do it gradually. And if we are clever enough we will make you feel that it was your idea in the first place to move, to change your wardrobe or to find another job.

This is how relationships should work: You change for us and we change for you if we feel that's what you want. Provided we really care about our relationship and we care about your feelings we will do this for you. So it actually works both ways.

Change in a relationship is a natural response to the needs of both partners in it. It is unusual for two people who really love each other to enter a relationship and remain unchanged. That kind of relationship is a sham, two people living together, carrying on with their separate lives much like they did before the relationship got started. It is, as you can imagine, a recipe for disaster.

People always complain that their partner doesn't love them the way they are or you can often hear a woman saying: "Why can't he love me for who I am?" Essentially the question perfectly illustrates a state of mind people have created in order to have a perfect excuse to do nothing and stay comfortable with who they are. We all change with time, our tastes change, our habits change, there is nothing in the world that doesn't change. So making an effort in a relationship is natural provided both people in the relationship are really interested in making it work.

Of course sometimes women go for a man who wasn't just 'hero' but was the choice of convenience and then they are trapped with a person they don't love and don't even feel attracted to. Then they try to change their men to be at least more likeable or more successful so being with him would become more bearable and that's when problems begin, particularly when you consider that in a situation like that, while they want him to change they are not really prepared to make any change in themselves, for him.

You see a woman needs to feel a lot of things about her man apart from love. We need to be proud of who you are, we need to respect you, we need to feel that you are the best you can be and if we don't feel all that just loving you sometimes is not enough.

When we feel that you won't change for us we immediately assume that you don't care about how we feel and that you don't care about the relationship itself.

I know I have said this before but, really, I cannot say it enough: relationships are full of compromises but it's always a two-way street. If she is trying to change you maybe you can make some sort of deal that could satisfy you both. Because if she is trying to change you she is unhappy and it is a problem you need to do something about as it's not going to go away by itself.

Doing nothing and hoping she'll get tired and give up is the worst possible thing you can do, because the moment this happens she has also given up on you and your being together and your relationship then, is on expiry notice, even if, outwardly, nothing appears to have changed.

Alisa Miller

#11. WHAT ARE YOU THINKING ABOUT?

We know it's silly to ask but we can't help ourselves and every time we see you thinking we ask the same odd question: What are you thinking about? And even when deeply inside we understand the whole ridiculousness of the question we simply can't stop asking that. Why?

Normally it happens when we are insecure about our relationship and more than anything we want to get inside your head and see how you feel about it. And because we think about it constantly ourselves we assume that you do the same thing, when, in reality, you are probably thinking about going to the pub with your friends or watching a game of football or just thinking about work.

Most of us don't actually get it. The fact that you can think about your friends or about an upcoming TV show right after sex for example can really hurt our feelings. Although we can sometimes be just as bad. But on the bright side you can always be sure about one thing when we do ask what you are thinking about we really do care about your thoughts and about you and are totally into you.

A woman who doesn't care about what's in your head is a woman who doesn't care about you. And although it can be incredibly frustrating and can annoy the hell out of you it's still a positive thing and you need to understand that.

IF IT GETS TOO MUCH

Granted this kind of intrusive questioning can get on your nerves. As a woman I totally understand that, just as I understand that most women simply cannot help themselves and will behave this way.

If you really want it to get better or even stop without hurting her feelings and without turning her off and putting your relationship on a rocky road try to make her feel secure about your relationship and tell her that she is in your thoughts all the time anyway and that she has nothing to worry about.

Explain to her that it's very difficult to always tell her what's on your mind and some thing should remain untold. If you manage to present it the right way she will eventually stop bothering you about it.

Or joke. Good joke always works. What are you thinking of? "The bees are disappearing and it really concerns me right this moment".

ON BEING HYSTERICAL

I know it's a 'joke'. Men always joke about women being hysterical in a sort of dismissive way which is usually intended to discount the seriousness of a request or an interaction or even an argument that's happened.

Because there is never smoke without a fire let's examine this a little. We do say things, you know, things we don't really mean but we can't help ourselves but spill it all out. In our heads things are associated. Because we notice things and know that they are all connected we tend to sometimes act or react in ways where what is happening is like a snowball coming down the mountain it just gets bigger with each passing second. It's when a small thing like forgetting something we told you suddenly becomes "You don't care about my feelings, you don't care about me!" and gets turned from something trivial into a relationship-defining issue.

Normally, you just need time to work things our in your head, some time alone to digest the argument and understand why it happened and why things escalated so fast. This usually means spending a little time alone because (let's face it) the reason things got out of hand is because of the way she made you react.

Unfortunately it works differently for her so the worst thing you could do is to leave her alone with her thoughts during the argument. In her mind it will only get bigger, nastier and so far off course that she will barely remember the point (or reason) where it all began. Inside her there will be nothing but fury, and misery and lots and lots of pain. Irascible? For sure it is, but that is also the way it is.

Never leave your woman alone with her thoughts during an argument – she may cool down but unless it has been resolved it will only be there to act as fuel for the next time there is an argument and it will be worse the next time. In a worst case scenario you are going to come back to a very angry woman and the argument is going to start all over again. We never think anything good while you are gone, we can just overcome it sometimes, but it doesn't leave our heads unless the problem has been resolved.

What a woman wants when there is an argument is to talk to you and work thing out there and then. The more you feel like running away the more she needs you to stay and tell her that you are never going to do just that or that whatever caused the issue to develop in the first place is not going to be an issue again. Not knowing is the worst thing that can happen to her and she hates it when you leave in order to 'cool down'.

The problems we have with you, as woman, when it comes to an argument, normally, are deeper than we say they are. We don't realize it when we start it, but eventually it all comes out. Most of the time, we are insecure and we need reassurance that it's all going the right way and you are the only person who can give us that reassurance.

I know this sounds a little weird for guys but that's how things are in a woman's head. Emotions drive us and sometimes they drive us mad. Your partner needs to spill it all out and unfortunately you are the only one who is around to take the brunt of it.

ADVICE

The best thing you can do when she gets hysterical is to listen. Listen to what she has to say, let her get it all out of her system and don't forget that half of the things she says when she is upset she doesn't even mean. She is having an overload and there is no other way to deal with it but to externalize it in a flow of words. Once she has finished just let her know that you care about her, tell her that no matter what everything can be fixed, lie if you have to and then she will calm down on her own and be reasonable when her brain has come out of the fog of hysteria. Right now she needs you to hold her and tell her that it's all going to be alright. Although she looks like a monster, she screams away and throws things at you deep inside all she needs is for you to hug her. 99% of the time it works. Beware of the 1% that's left though.

#12.
EXCITEMENT IN HER LIFE

It's true to say that everyone needs a little dose of excitement now and then. Excitement is a fragile thing; it's here today and tomorrow it's gone and you have no idea how it happened. Women are addicted to excitement; they need passion in their lives. Why do you think women are so much into romances and soap operas? It gives us the ultimate adventure, we experience passion, danger, rick and romance while it's safe and secure in real life (and yet so boring!).

As time passes you may feel she is not as excited about sex, she is not so excited about seeing you, she is not so excited about you. Yes, she smiles, she jokes and fools around, she makes love but at the same time she seems distant, disengaged. If that's what you perceive this is exactly what is happening. She has no excitement in her life and this is why she can't enjoy life itself.

Routine kills passion faster than a bullet and day after day she feels less and less for you slowly getting used to the idea of you, the sense of always you being there, sorting things out. You become some sort of fixed point in her life. She doesn't feel like talking to you about things unless it's gossip or something she needs to get done. She vanishes in books, movies, or even other people. She needs to feel something stronger, a sense that life has not simply passed her by and this is the case when love is not enough or even worse love has been overtaken by boredom and nothing much remains.

This is exactly the reason why we like bad guys. They are unpredictable, they can blow our minds any time with excitement, a sense of the adventure and a sense of the forbidden, and we can never say for sure what they are going to do next. Excitement can be so addictive that sometimes we simply can't live without it and look for it anywhere we can.

ADVICE
If you want her to adore you make her feel WOW. Be unpredictable, surprise her every now and then and you will see how much difference it makes to the way she reacts to you. Women get incredibly bored with their domesticated husbands and can often get involved with other men simply because they want some excitement in their lives.

If you want to make her feel adventurous think about: Taking her away for a magic night at the hotel without notice and go wild once you are there with her.

Make her feel wanted.

Do the unexpected. Even things you may feel are too silly and unimaginative are actually the things she is hoping you are going to think about. Like singing a serenade under her balcony or bringing her coffee in bed in the morning. You see, maybe it's not reinventing the wheel but it's her wheel and that's what makes it special.

Don't forget the romance! Women love to be rescued and fought for.

Alisa Miller

#13. WHY DOES SHE IGNORE YOU?

When a girl ignores you it really does mean something. Some girls just hope you'll take the hint. You know, we are not very good at playing all these games sometimes although we know them all. If we really like you we will never lose your phone number or forget we agreed to meet you. You see, if she is not very keen on going anywhere with you or keeps moving the date and "something just keeps coming up" it's what it is, she is not interested in you.

Don't be mistaken when she spends time talking to you on the phone or texting you from time to time as we, women, just do these things. We would talk to you forever because we simply can't get rid of you instead of telling you straight away that we are not into you. We know that it's better to be honest but some of us just can't do it because we do not really want o hurt your feelings so we spend time with you and suffer. Till it gets too much and we finally spell it out for you.

Sometimes we use you. Unfortunately we see it as "no harm done" since you like it when we are around you anyway. We use you when we are feeling low and we need to tell ourselves that we are still in demand and that someone still likes us and feels attracted to us. We text you when we are feeling low or when we simply want to kill time waiting for an appointment at the dentist. We can even be cruel and try to show you off to our friends as a lap pet ready to rush the second we ask for it.

In general this is just the way it is. She is not going to like you unless she finds that you have something worth spending her time to explore.

I'll tell you a secret: women like men they have to fight for. We find them irresistible.

ADVICE

If she ignores you it's very difficult at that point to regain her interest but not impossible. Here is the plan: You need to look at yourself realistically and see if there is something which needs changing. Don't tell me there isn't and that you are perfect the way you are. Come on, you have seen all those Make Over reality TV shows! There is always room for improvement. Find ways to improve the way you look.

You need to make sure she knows that you are actually interested in somebody else. You need to tell her that you need advice on this new love of yours. Make sure you have something to back it up with. Like an email or text messages. You can even ask one of your friends to play the part when she is around.

Show her the time of her life but be distant. Establish a friendly relationship with her and then slowly feed her with details about your new relationship. Show her that you are in demand.

But never waste your time on expensive gifts or romantic letters if she is already ignoring you. She will only feel sorry for you and this is not the reaction any man would want. In order to get her interest back you need to work really hard for her to believe that you are worth it. You need to make her believe that you have moved on for a start and don't want her anymore; show her that you are in demand and you have yet many surprises up your sleeve.

#14. HOW TO INTEREST HER

Women are always aware of every little thing and that's a fact. We notice things you would never have thought anybody can possibly notice and things that on the surface, at least, appear to not matter much. Women notice everything especially you, men.

She sees you and she judges you. She looks at the way you handle yourself, the way you look and talk, the value you possibly have, how interesting you are and most importantly if any other woman has noticed you and paid attention. She will always be interested in attracting a man other women want. And even if she doesn't look interested at all she might be working out the plan on how on can she get closer to you right this minute.

On the other hand she may really be not interested. We, women, are really funny creatures, if we feel you are not worth our attention we won't bother. And in order to interest her you need to have the following: A few other girls at your feet already (if you have that, ignore all the rest).

Brad Pitt looks.

An expensive car (that's a 50/50 gamble – she may think it's your dad's).

A line that will be just right for the moment, intriguing and interesting without being corny.

Provided you have something interesting about you, you have enough confidence and you are not afraid to go to her first she will definitely notice you.

HER BODY LANGUAGE WHEN SHE IS BORED

Even when a woman is not interested in you and quite likely not very interested in what you are saying she will probably still try and make an effort to listen to you and look interested. The reasons are various but mostly she is trying to be polite.

If she is biting her lower lip that means she wants to say something but can't find the right moment and you are still talking.

If you feel that you are losing eye contact with her but she is still nodding and making agreeing sounds you probably have already lost her and she is failing to concentrate on your words. She is looking away in desperation, subconsciously trying to escape from you. Something is probably occupying her thoughts at that point and unfortunately it's more important than what you are saying. But don't attack her with accusations of not paying attention or being disinterested. After all she did make an effort to show you the opposite.

If you want to get her attention back ask her about how she is doing or change the subject starting with "Anyway, how is ..." switching to something you know she has a real interest in. The point is that, at that moment, physically she is there with you. Use the opportunity to get her interest back and win her over.

You can also tell if she is bored if her foot is tapping the floor when she is sitting down. It's a subconscious attempt to run away.

She is bored when she is playing with her mobile pressing buttons without intending to use it, blocking and unblocking the keypad.

Naturally our body language is easy to read as that's how we let you know how we feel without saying a word. It's the way we communicate at a subliminal, animal level and instinctively you should be able to read it. For instance in the way we sit there are open positions, closed positions; positions which let you know how we feel about you or the situation. If she seems to be sitting or standing sideways to you she is probably feeling like going away. If she is looking straight at you and her body is positioned directly at you she is interested in what you've got to say.

She is pretty bored if she doesn't smile or her smile feels unnatural or if she starts checking her nails. You can always spot if she is bored with what you are saying you just need to see if she is paying attention or if it feels like she is waiting for you to finish so she can get up and go.

If she doesn't ask questions and just does a lot of nodding she is probably waiting for you to stop so she can move on without appearing rude. If you want her to stay and talk you will need to change the subject into one which is more likely to interest her (like talking about her and her life for example) and stay alert to the signals she is sending so you can fine-tune the conversation.

Alisa Miller

HER BODY LANGUAGE WHEN SHE IS INTERESTED IN YOU

As we saw earlier we, women, compete for any man worth competing for in a room with other women just because we need to feed our ego. Unfortunately it won't necessarily mean we are going to go any further with it but you will, at least, know we were interested. It works for all of us: happily married, single, divorced, with partners or lovers; we all do it anyway just to prove to ourselves we can have you. It might be simply useful to know that we did try and check if you notice us just so you know we did.

The million dollar question here is how will you know that she is interested in you?

Well, you will know she is interested in you because she won't be completely relaxed, her posture will be a little bit made-up: she will arch her back, she will make sure she looks good and her clothes look perfect. She may even check her face in a mirror or ask her friend if her make up is alright. You will catch her looking at you briefly from time to time – she will be checking to see if her efforts are being appreciated.

If she is available the brief checking on you won't stop when she'll catch you looking back at her. Normally for any woman who is not available and who is just scoring points to prove to herself that she can attracts attention this is the end of it – once she catches you looking at her with interest she loses hers and will not look at you again. She has done her bit here (I know it's confusing but we really are complicated creatures).

You can always tell if a woman is interested in you. But you can rarely tell straight away if it's a serious interest or it is just a game. If she is interested for whatever reason she will make sure she will position herself where you can see her. She will make sure her hair is perfect: she may try to touch it or shake it or bury her hand in it if it's long enough.

She will wet her lips. There are different ways she can achieve that: she can simply lick them but these days we get lipsticks with watery effect so she may simply make sure that hers is still there by biting her lips or putting some more of it on, she may even have a drink so some of it will stay on her lips making them wet. It's something we do unconsciously and are programmed to do by nature.

Alisa Miller

#15. HER PSYCHOLOGY - TALKING TRASH

What is the main difference between a man and a woman? Well, there is an obvious one I am sure I do not need to explain to you in detail, the one I am talking about here is the way we use communication.

Most of our problems come from misinterpreting each other's words. Men never say anything without a reason or without a purpose while women do that all the time. We say things that just pop into our heads jumping from one subject to the other at the speed of light. We can talk for hours about nothing and yet it would feel like we talked pretty much about everything. Why do we do your brains in with all this then? Don't we understand that you don't care about somebody else's haircut or that somebody's sister has a new boyfriend? Well, we don't. We honestly don't. For us it's not just words, we feel that this way we share part of ourselves and our inner world.

We feel that that's what we supposed to do with you, our man. We feel that we have to share our whole world with you. We think that we absolutely have to describe every second of our day to you and make sure we haven't missed a detail. Most of us don't actually realize how annoying it can be loading you with all the (in your eyes only) rubbish we just read in a magazine or heard on TV.

Normally we don't even realize that we can give you the impression that you have to do something about the information we have just given you. And sometimes we may even mislead you with what we are saying. It's important that you understand that most of the things we say are just thoughts said aloud and they don't require any action from you and sometimes they don't even require you paying much attention to what we say. Although we would crucify you if we find out you don't. So – be warned.

ADVICE
To play it safe simple remember to insert some "Huh-huh" and "Oh really" and maybe "Yeah, that's not good" while we are talking away. We won't even notice you have no idea what we are talking about. We won't even remember what we were talking about in the next fifteen minutes but we will remember if we catch you not caring about what we say because then it means that you don't care about us.

Yep, we actually will really think that if you blow up or tell us "Oh you are talking trash again". We then hear that you don't care about us and our

Alisa Miller

feelings. We will suspect that you don't care about our thoughts because you don't love us. But that follows shortly after the non-caring faze anyway. We will be get hurt and make sure you know about it - immediately.

We talk to you about what may look like to be like nothing but it means a lot not in what we say but why we say all these things. By talking to you we share our thoughts and that means we are sharing ourselves. Well, maybe not every second thought we say aloud is something of high value and they may not be scientifically valid at all but how many genius thoughts do you generate per second yourself? It's actually hard work to generate as much trash per second as we do.

But what happens if we stop talking? You will probably feel relieved. But it's not really good news. If we stopped talking to you about things we care about, then it means we don't want to share anymore.

And this also means that the door to our world is just about to close for you. For women it's actually much easier to give you their body than their mind. Being in her thoughts, in her head and in her heart - this is a real challenge for every man. It's easy to find a man we would just sleep with but it's much harder to find one who will listen to us. If you listen long enough (without going brain dead) we will start trusting you with more serious things. Like out feelings and our dreams.

It's official that there is no sisterhood. So practically no woman on earth really has a friend. Yes, each one of us has a best friend and maybe a sister, mothers sometimes make good friends. But in reality all we want is to have a man who could be our friend as well as our lover.

In most cases we can just find one or the other. So you see when you think we are just loading you with trash, we are honestly thinking we are sharing our thoughts. Even the most intelligent of us sometimes need that dummy offload to get rid of some steam or to share the information we are excited about. It's important you don't take anything of it too seriously. In most cases our words don't require any action from you. Make sure we think you are listening and you'll be alright.

Alisa Miller

#16. WHY DOES SHE COMPLAIN?

Why would anybody complain? You only do that when you feel it will make a difference otherwise what's the point of wasting breath, right? Well, when it comes to a woman complaining it's more about getting rid of the emotions and negative feelings she has inside her.

Women, unlike men, are not very good in dealing with their emotions and when they feel insecure, helpless or feel that the whole world is crushing them they need to talk to someone.

Normally, what you'll hear is all the negative stuff which is more likely to sound like a complaint. So when you think your girlfriend or wife is constantly complaining she is actually trying to share her feelings with you. Well, negative feelings anyway. Unfortunately most women can't feel the difference between a complaint and sharing and can nag you to death when they don't get the desirable reaction.

When you hear her complaining what's your first thought? If you're like some of the male friends I have it is most probably: "She's doing it again. How can I make her stop?" And the first action is to try and find the solution to her problem whatever it is because then you feel you have fulfilled your part of the bargain in your relationship.

If she is feeling that she is failing as a mother you try to take the kid off her mind or if she is tired and complaining about the housework or her parents you are trying to take care of it too by taking the pressure off her. It works but it's not what she needs.

Women may be emotional and "share" a lot of their problems with you but generally have quite a lot of stamina when it comes to bearing up with and adapting to situations. Most of us do, anyway. So when she is telling you how bad her day was or she is frustrated with the dirty carpet all she wants is for you to tell her that it's going to be ok.

And that's it. She doesn't want you to be a superman rushing to deal with all her problems. What she really wants is Clark Kent to hold her hand, hug and reassure her that it's all going to be Ok. And suddenly problems at work, broken down washing machines and annoying neighbors don't seem to matter that much anymore. You can't imagine what one supportive word can do to a woman who finds herself feeling some despair.

And we do despair a lot. It doesn't mean we can't deal with our own troubles ourselves. We can and we will. And it's important that you don't just solve everything for us because at some point we will get used to you fixing every little thing at our first request. We get spoiled and learn to rely on you for everything. And we feel, at that point, that if you fail to fix something you are a traitor and a bastard.

Give us the reassurance that things are going to get better, offer us your help but don't just take care of everything for us – you are not doing us a favor.

A woman needs a friend more then she needs a lover. She needs someone whom she can rely on when things get tough. She needs to know that you'll be there for her when she needs you. If it's a small thing like a broken nail (man laugh and underestimate its importance to a woman's mind) or a huge one like her beloved grandmother's death. If you feel she cares about something deeply and you can see she is very unhappy about it no matter how ridiculous or silly it may seem you need to offer her your support. And she'll be happy like a child.

You've no doubt heard women saying that they need a 'sensitive' man. You might then have imagined in your mind's eye, the kind of man who wears Speedos and eyeliner. But when a woman says she needs a sensitive man she means that she needs someone who'll be sensitive towards her feelings. It doesn't mean that you really have to understand why she feels so bad when someone just bought the last handbag she wanted for herself. It is a small and ridiculous thing from your point of view but if it makes her upset it doesn't matter how ridiculous it may seem you need to show your understanding and your support.

We women get upset over a lot of things as we are naturally more emotional then you. We find it difficult to deal with our feelings on our own and we tend to share them with the rest of the world and normally the primary target is you. When you fail to understand how frustrated we are that we don't have a nail polish which matches our lipstick and we've only discovered this an hour before going out we feel you don't support us and you are being insensitive. And you think we are just crazy.

We get upset and we complain although we don't actually realize we are getting on your nerves. From our point of view we are expressing our feelings aloud. It may sound like a joke to you but this is actually exactly the way we feel about it. Once you understand our psychology and the way we deal with our thoughts by saying it all out loud it will be really easy for you to be around us and stop suffering.

There is a rule for every woman's complaint that works like magic. All you need to do is to tell her that you understand and support her, that it's going to be alright. At the end of the day that's ALL we want from you. We don't really expect you to understand why we get upset or frustrated, the only reason we say we are is for you to tell us that it's not a big deal and things will work out. There will be new handbag in the store, we look fantastic even without any makeup on at all, that there will be a better brighter day tomorrow and what is really important that you are there for us.

Alisa Miller

#17. WHY DOES SHE HATE YOUR FRIENDS?

The number of times I have seen relationships which looked promising break up because a woman did not like the company her man kept indicate that there is a problem which happens again and again in relationships.

The question here is why? Why would she hate your friends so much? Well, we always do if we feel that your friends are a threat. If we feel or even know that your friends don't like us we will try to make you stop seeing them completely.

We know very well how these men-gatherings work, and how you relax and discuss women, other women, the glory days of being free and being able to hit on all these women. We understand that this kind of influence is going to eventually make you take their side and take you away from us.

But more than anything we are very scared that at some point there will be a moment when you will listen to your friends and their advice. And if you are not 100% happy with us you will listen to what they have to say. What we are really afraid of then is that you will give them the basis to give you advice on our relationship. You will tell them that you are unhappy or that we are not as good as you would want us to be. We are afraid that being away from us with your friends you are capable of doing things you would never do without them. We are afraid that they are going to take you away from us.

So every time you go away we wait and hold our breath and hope that your friends won't turn you against us. How do we know they do that? Because this is what we do for our own friends. When two friends who trust each other get together all the problems and all the secrets come out.

We hate them because you trust them more then us. We hate them because with them you can have fun without making an effort and we hate them because you enjoy their company. When with us it's always an effort and you always need to try really hard and watch what you are saying. We know that we can't compete here and the only way we can stop being constantly afraid of their influence on you is to make you see them as little as possible or not at all.

In reality it's nothing more than a battle for your full attention and a case of pure envy that they get something from you we feel we can never have: the happy, natural you. We feel that your friends are stealing you from us, your precious time which you could have spent with us, doing things for us and our relationship.

HOW TO DEAL WITH IT?
It's very difficult to make the woman in your life feel safe when it comes to your meeting with friends she doesn't know or she's not sure about in gatherings she doesn't attend.

The best way of dealing with it is to make your friends her friends too. That way she doesn't need to wonder what's going on when you meet up because she will be there to witness it. In a best case scenario she will realize that your friends are not a threat and she will leave you alone. But this doesn't work for everyone.

Unfortunately if she really doesn't like your friends she will make you get rid of them one way or another. You can try and make her feel secure and tell her that you understand why she is being so unreasonable, that you understand her fear and jealousy, and she hasn't got anything to worry about because whatever your friends say you love her and it cannot be changed.

Every time you come back make her feel that you are happy to be back to her, tell her everything about your meeting in great detail so she will feel that you trust her and put her above your friendship by giving all your buddies up to her (in a manner of speaking).

#18. THE MONTHLY MONSTER

Don't you wonder why suddenly from nowhere every month your gentle flower of a girlfriend suddenly turns into a moody monster? Unfortunately this is something we can't really control and this is individual to each one of us.

We can't control our hormones and once in a while we do feel like ripping the world apart and every little thing suddenly becomes big in our heads. There is no cure and the only way to be safe here is to know when your girlfriend has her period and make sure you are nowhere around her and if you are brave enough you can try to help her with your support.

Normally we overreact. It's not a myth or an overstatement as hormones can do that to us. It feels like evil takes over and at that point we are no longer in control. Thankfully it doesn't last for a very long time and soon enough we are already apologizing for our behavior.

Women do suffer a lot during their period. Before it even starts some of us get spots and/or a terrible pain in our lower abdomen. Then we are worried every month if it's late or terrified if it comes too early and we are unprepared. Our skin smell changes and we also feel uncomfortable generally. Of course we won't tell you that, it's bad enough you have to deal with having no sex for a week.

Bad as they are, periods, are always better than the alternative, unless of course you are ready to start seeing your 'tribe' increase in size.

#19. WHY IS SHE ADDICTED TO SHOPPING?

Women are easily addicted to anything easily accessible to them which will make them feel good about themselves.

Things like food and clothes shopping for example can make her happy instantly without applying any extra effort or at least, it feels this way. We use food as a pain killer, for comfort and a sort of shelter but once it gets too much and we understand that it's going to make us fat and unattractive we quit; but the addiction to comfort and satisfaction is still there.

For a woman being beautiful is everything, being shiny new and sparkling is something every one of us wants as long as we are interested in attracting attention from the opposite sex.

Alisa Miller

We see clothes as a get-there-fast solution and although you don't really care what we wear as long as we look hot in it we do need to have a sense of change and style and fashion.

We need new clothes, new pieces in our wardrobe to feel all new ourselves. We feel that if we will get that dress we are going to look like the model wearing it when most of the times we are buying the look and not the dress itself.

Every little piece of material makes us feel different, it can makes us feel special and this is why it's so addictive, this is why we follow fashion to be up to date and to be noticed. It's not like we need every other man to fall on his knees and whisper "gosh, she is wearing Armani!" but we love it when men turn their heads when we pass by.

Unfortunately as any addiction it tends to go too far for most of its victims. Addicted to shopping we stop understanding why we actually shop. Most of the times we shop for things that supposedly are going to make us feel better, to help us change and make our life change for the better.

Some of us go into house (appliance & furniture) shopping because it makes us feel we can control things around us just like we used to control our own appearance. Things are just things but not for someone who is desperate in a situation of not having control of anything but the house. Controlling our environment and the things around us, controlling the material things surrounding us makes us feel good but unfortunately not for long as that feeling doesn't last. So we are trapped inside a shopping mall for as long as we have money to spend. And then again, after we are home and the feeling wears off, the need to shop starts all over again.

Men say that women are full of insecurities. And they are right. Insecurity drives us through most of our life and for some of us it really is a pretty miserable existence. We shop, we buy, we spend but it all eventually ends in realization that we can't really make anything work, we can't make things fit and we certainly can't make ourselves look like a model by just buying that dress.

We are addicted to upgrades essentially. We will repaint the house, buy a new vase, order a new dress and a couple of belts and we will be happy, or at least in that particular moment we will be happy. But once the euphoria of buying is gone we need something new and we need it right now. And as good as we felt buying something the time before now we need the feeling just as strong if not stronger. It's like getting high with a greater and greater input required each time.

When we can't eat we look at food, when we can't buy clothes, we window shop just as miserable as it makes us not buying anything, having it all will not makes us any happier. It all comes down to feeling that we can't be happy in any other way and this is where we go wrong. Shopping is easy, we go to the shop and we buy. But working towards real long-term happiness is something much harder to do and each one of us knows that. Sometimes we are not sure ourselves what can make us happy so get 'high' by constantly consuming.

ADVICE
If a woman you care about is addicted to shopping it's not because she has no brains whatsoever but because she doesn't know any better and she needs help. It's an addiction and it needs to be treated as such.

Alisa Miller

If you make her feel secure and loved, if you give her something else that will make her feel good and make her open up as a person, she'll find something that makes her happy and it hasn't got a price tag and this will go a long way towards weaning her off her shopping addiction.

Essentially we all, men and women, want the same thing; we all want to be happy. We all try to find our place and have a life searching for the right way or at least the one that will make us feel good and it's only limited by our morals and prejudices.

At least shopping doesn't kill anyone... and it doesn't make us fat and if money is not an issue, as addictions go, it's fairly harmless.

#20. HOW IMPORTANT IS MONEY TO HER?

When we came out of the caves and met other humans we had something we could trade which was based strictly on goods we had and goods we needed.

When we met more humans with different goods, some of which we had probably not even imagined, trading became more complex and there was the need to have something universal and something easy to carry for trading in other regions.

As we developed this universal measure developed with us but it still remained just as it was back then in a stone age: food, clothes and shelter.

I am here, as you probably guess, glossing over huge tracts of cultural, anthropological and social development in order to make a point: Money now and money then performs the same function: it is

Alisa Miller

vital for survival just like hunting a mammoth and bringing it home to your family. So how important do you think it is? The man who can hunt more and bring more was considered to be a good option for a woman back then. Seen in this context it becomes quite natural for women to be attracted to men with money and the cliché phrase: "she is after him because he earns a lot of money" begins to take, suddenly, an entirely different hue.

Whether like it or not women always will be after the strongest men we can find. Of course, it doesn't mean we will put money before our heart but it also doesn't mean we are not going to think about it first. Money is important to everyone, women, men, and especially needed where children and elderly people are concerned and just because saying it out loud is not something everyone wants to hear it doesn't mean we can all pretend it isn't important.

Yet again, as women, we trade beauty for money, money for beauty over and over again. Having a lot of money, as a man, gives you a bigger variety of women ready to give you their beauty in return while having no money whatsoever limits your chances dramatically.

Women are not exactly driven by money when they are looking for a partner but then again money can play a role as an accelerator when it comes to moving forward with someone in particular. It's not about having a great lifestyle (although that wouldn't hurt either) it's about having a secure future. It's a logical choice for a woman to get as much as she can when she can with a man who can give it to her. You can be as bitter as you want but that is just the way things work.

We don't mind you being poor we will still love you all the same. What we object to is your willingness to do nothing about it and make us take your side on that score. We can't stand passive men and men who are quite happy where they are and we will make sure you know our position and remind you on a daily basis. We are not bitchy and we are not money-hungry, we are simply afraid that we made the wrong choice by listening to our heart for too long.

If you are bright and you are willing to go out there and hunt us a fine mammoth even though you are as poor as a church mouse right now we will worship you because that will leave us hope that things will change. But if we see you lying on the sofa all day long for years we'll keep cursing the day we met you.

Money is not *the* most important thing for us in life, we would rather spend our life with a man who really understands and cherishes us than with a rich man, but it is worth bearing in mind that having enough money is hugely important to us as it provides us with security. Nature has made us this way. We are bad mammoths hunters ourselves and, as such, we have no choice but to hunt the hunters.

Alisa Miller

#21. WHAT IMPRESSES HER?

What do you think "impresses women"? Do you think it's big cars with tinted windows? Champaign with caviar on board of a jet or a 20 carat diamond?

The truth is that a woman is easy to impress even if you haven't got a lot of money. What really impresses us is a confident men you don't meet very often these days. Nothing impresses us more than a man who knows what he is doing.

Every girl dreams of a superman, the one who is not afraid of anything, and the one who always knows what to do. That does impress, especially these days when we see more men being afraid of mice and being concerned about messing up their hair when this is strictly a woman's prerogative. Being a man in the full meaning of the word can impress any woman!

Women are convinced that confidence comes with experience and having a strong character and even when they are not completely convinced about this, a confident man will always intrigues them.

As a man, the more you show her that you know what you are doing and where you are going the more impressed she will get with you.

There is nothing which can dampen a woman's appetite more and cool her passion than a complaining man. He is practically taking the only thing we are good at away from us. A confident man, by contrast, acts as a woman-magnet and the more you're in demand the more we want you, naturally fighting for the best mate for us out there.

There is a need to clarify this a little here. By confident I am not talking about confidence in the way you look or in how fast you can get us to sleep with you. The confidence I am talking about is related to your actions and your plans and the way you generally handle yourself and those around you and it barely involves us.

Women are very good at spotting the vibes gives off by a truly confident man. We judge you by the way you interact with the world and then decide if we are impressed with you or not. We won't take the bait of you telling us how good you are in bed or how rich your dad is but we will react immediately if we see you are a man who knows what he is doing with his life. That's why we are impressed if you tell us you are a doctor for example because to us that means that you are not just saving people but you have a purpose in your life which has taken planning, dedication and perseverance to get you there.

When you approach us in a bar and you mumble and look shifty, no matter how well dressed you might be, it will put us off you. We are interested in who you are and what you have to offer and if you panic over anything for longer than for two seconds you get into our blacklist of losers and we lose interest in you.

Women are easy to understand and impress once you realize what really drives us. Essentially it's the same thing for all of us: we all want to find a partner, a strong and confident man who can take care of us and secure our future. Once you get this everything else is just details and you can work other thing out with time.

#22. WHY IS SHE ALWAYS LATE?

We are all familiar with the popular media picture of a man's ritual for going out coming down to his picking a shirt up from a pile and sniff it to see if it is good enough to do the trick.

When a woman is getting ready to go out however she needs to make sure: that her make up is perfect, that it looks in daylight just as good as it does in the bathroom mirror, that the nail polish she has matches the dress she is wearing, that the dress is not the same she wore yesterday, that her period is still a week away, that her handbag has everything she can possibly need should she get stranded on a desert island with Brad Pitt and she usually has to get all this done in 10 minutes because she is already late for her date with you.

You see it's not easy being a girl. You always complain that you need to shave 10 minutes every morning, when we need at least an hour in order to do it (legs, armpits and bikini line), put our make up on and dry our hair.

Every little thing, when done properly, takes forever and the list of things we need to do before you see us is endless. It takes only one of these things to go wrong and the whole chain of events falls apart and we are definitely are going to be late by an hour.

Beyond the preparation required for us to be totally satisfied with the results of our beauty regime, there is also the preconception that a woman needs to be a little bit late in order to avoid appearing over-eager. We do take our time because we know we can and that you will forgive us.

Have you ever woken up next to a girl who the night before looked radiant and beautiful and seen her first thing in the morning? Most of us look like ghosts if not worse. Centuries of perfecting and working out the procedures required to make us beautiful have also turned us into the slaves of our own expectations. We can't imagine going out without having full makeup on, and our hair nicely done. And all this takes forever especially when we remember we haven't done something at the last moment, on the way out and need to go back in and rectify it.

#23. HOW TO MAKE HER HAPPY

Men have this idea of a perfect way to make a woman happy and it usually requires a lot of money being spend and when you don't have it you just give up trying.

I know I have already mentioned that money is important to a woman but that is a long-term consideration and it comes into play in terms of a woman seeing you as being capable of making money, rather than being rich right now.

In reality we don't need you to throw a one-in-a-life-time party for us so we can be happy. Happiness comes from being satisfied with life and yourself and it has very little to do with money.

I will grant you that with women especially it's difficult to guess as we seem to confuse "need" and "want" on a daily basis. Yet there are some things you can apply to any woman and using these guidelines you can make any of us the happiest woman on Earth.

There are two types of happiness: happiness in the moment and long-term happiness. It's easy to make her jump on the spot from happiness by just buying her something she wanted for a long time (like a pair of designer shoes). But it's the long-term feeling of happiness that is tricky and unfortunately it cannot be bought no matter how much money you have got to spare.

In order for her to be absolutely happy she needs to have stability in her life and feel that she is loved (and will be loved as time passes), she needs to be able to rely on someone (you) and have room for self-realization and mistakes without feeling she is under pressure and fighting for survival all the time.

This formula is guaranteed to make her happy permanently: Love + Security + Self-Realization = Happiness.

It begs a few questions like How to make her feel secure? Normally it's about marriage but not necessarily so all the time. If you make sure you tell her enough times that she is the only one in your life and there is no one who can match her in any way eventually she will start believing you (as you already know most of the time we don't trust a word you say unless you've already said it 1000 times before). So be patient and keep repeating it, eventually we will understand and stop worrying about what's going to happen tomorrow. Just keep telling her: I will love you all the same when you are 90 (needs to be repeated at least 5000 times). I love the way you look and I absolutely adore your body (nothing short of 3000 will do here). I can't see anyone else but you, other women don't exist for me

(50 times should do it – we want to believe it so much). You know you can always rely on me no matter what happens (repeat 500 times), I will love you the same even if you get fat[1] (repeat 3500 times) My friends are less important to me than you (repeat 500 times), I don't care what my mum says about you I will never leave you or love you any less (repeat 1600 times), I have never seen a woman more beautiful than you (repeat at least 2000 times).

The numbers in brackets are my own invention and there is no science behind them but believe me when I say we, women, really need to hear these again and again, it's a real need for us and we are addicted to it.

This also brings up the question on how to help her with self-realization? Most of us are generally very insecure about everything: our looks, our abilities, our talents even if we look like we don't give a damn we are simply hiding it well. So we are in desperate need of a lot of praise and inspiring words. And this is where it becomes a full time job for you because we need a lot of it and we need it on a daily basis.

We need you to tell us that we are great, that we are talented and we can do anything. Once again like with anything else it only takes a few thousand times of hearing the same thing again and again and eventually we start to think it's true. Your support

---

[1] Be careful with this one because she may actually relax and get fat. Make sure you add: "But I know you won't you are too beautiful to let yourself go". Still it's the one line worth lying about as it will defiantly make her happy even if she knows it's a lie.

and your inspiring words can make any woman happy because essentially that's what we want from you anyway. Most of the time we don't care how good you are in bed if you make us feel good about ourselves the rest of the time.

See clothes and jewelry don't make us happy, they just make us pleased because we feel you find us worth spending lots of money on. Gifts really are important because that's how we know you are still in love with us and you still spend time and money on finding something that will please us. But true happiness is far from materialistic and unfortunately for you it takes time and patience. What you say to us and the way you react to us is what makes us truly happy.

If you say we look lovely, we start shining and dancing, if you don't notice a new hairstyle or a new dress we feel we have failed and all we want to do now is hide. Compliments and praise is a fuel for every woman's beauty and it acts like an accelerator on the way to happiness.

#24.
FAITHFULNESS AND INFIDELITY

Earlier I told you about two women competing over the attention of a guy in one room with them, even through it was not necessarily leading anywhere. I showed you how important it is for a woman to be better than her competitor, the other woman.

When it comes to the question of fidelity it gets tougher and much more brutal. The way women see it they have to claim their man and then protect him the same way American ranchers protect their land. Don't you feel the same way about your woman? It's about ownership and it's about trust. Although we tend to use term "partnership" instead of "ownership" at the end of the day this is exactly what it is if you are married or even if you are just officially dating. There are rules and they are very clear: you don't have any romantic or sexual relationship with anyone else but your partner.

When it comes to women unless they don't care about their men (but sometimes even then) their partner's fidelity is the number one rule that cannot be negotiated. It's never about sex but always about betrayal as by having sex with someone else you basically saying that you wanted someone else.

This is where it all gets funny. These days because we talk about affairs a lot no one actually thinks about it long enough to understand how truly deep the problem is here. Sex may not last very long in most cases but for that short time you do want the person you are having sex with and this is when you break the special bond you have between you and your partner.

Being faithful is what every woman wants from you because that proves that she is the one you want. It's that simple. And this is why we take your affair as a sign of the end of the relationship and we understand that there can no longer be any trust between us.

You men think that just looking at and not touching another woman is not a big deal. Unfortunately it is. You see admitting you like other women is just as bad as having sex with them it's just we can't take any action on that one as there was no line crossed for the storm to come. But it hurts just as much. How would you feel about us wanting other men? Checking out their asses? Wouldn't you be hurt? But traditionally we try and fix the relationship if that happens as long as there was no physical intercourse we still hope that things can be fixed.

You being with another woman is your partner's worst nightmare because that would mean that there are other women for you and that she is not safe, she is not guarded and she is not loved anymore.

A lot of couples try to start their relationship from the beginning if one of the partners has had an affair, they try to fix things and stay together. But it's like trying to fix a broken vase it may look whole but it will have visible cracks and you will know that it was broken. Normally we are afraid of change and for us having a bad relationship is better than having none at all and because with years people get too used to each other so much it's difficult to then suddenly walk away.

In every case for both of men and women it's not about sex when we go with another person outside the relationship we have. It's always a signal that we have a problem, much deeper problem than we realize. And since sex is not that important to us women having an affair with someone else is about feeling wanted and not about the actual act itself.

Whether we like it or not being unfaithful is the end of the relationship. And no matter how hard we try to fix it afterwards, it will never be the same and it will never quite work as there always will be a note of mistrust and suspicion tainting every moment.

It's all about attention at the end of the day. The way we women see it is all your attention has to be concentrated on us. We see everybody else men and other women especially as a threat and we treat them accordingly. We will object to you helping another woman or even being nice to her even if you didn't even have any thoughts at the back of your money or any ulterior motives and the strength of our objection will be proportionate to the measure of our trust in you.

Even if we trust you completely we will still notice and question why you reacted to another woman and how much of a threat she is to us no matter how brief and meaningless your attention was in your own eyes.

So if you do like other women and if you notice them make sure she doesn't see it and doesn't even suspect it or you'll be in trouble one way or another.

She can never know that you even look at other women never mind entertaining the possibility that you might want them. It's like a pint of poison to her to realize that there is a possibility no matter how slight in which you can be taken away from her maybe not today but tomorrow.

When you feel that she is trying to get attention from other men and she really cares how they react you need to be extremely careful how you go about it.

It's quite natural for both members of both sexes to flirt and feed their egos but how we do it and how we work around our relationship makes all the difference.

Just needing the attention and just feeling other people are excited about us is very different to wanting them. Woman's nature is to try and get the attention of every (good) male to secure her chances of survival (i.e. having a man by her side) and to prove that she can have a man anytime is very important to her ego and self-esteem.

Why do we object? Because sometimes you don't see the difference between us fishing for other man's attention and you looking at other women. When you do that you actually want them and when we try to get attention from other men that is exactly what we want just the attention and we don't want the men, for us it's a game and nothing more.

Unless of course we do want other men. But then wouldn't you be the first to know this? If we make an effort for other men and we don't make the same effort for you there is something seriously wrong with the relationship we are in and before it's too late we do need to talk about it.

Sex outside the relationship is never just sex. Normally it's the last and final step to say that it's over between you and her.

Alisa Miller

#25. MAKING AND BREAKING PROMISES

If you think that we record every word you say you are right because we do. And everything you promise us we record it twice constantly checking on it and making sure that you are going to keep your word. Unfortunately it's in our nature to be constantly afraid you are going to trick us. And it doesn't matter how big or how small the promise is, like taking the trash out or being with us for the rest of our life, we will hold on to it with the same force and come down on you like a ton of bricks if you fail to deliver.

When you make a promise you need to understand that on the receiving side she will be waiting for it to materialize and she won't forget. That every day, every minute you will delay she will count it against you. It has nothing to do with her being vindictive and writing things down so that later she can score points. No, she is waiting like a child for you to not betray her expectations.

When you make a promise sometimes you make it just to keep her calm and stop her from getting on your nerves. It's quite understandable but there is one mistake you can never make in a case like that: you never give her the date when you are going to keep your promise unless you are going to stick to it. She will wait, patiently, she will hold on to that date waiting, long after you have forgotten.

And when you think she will understand you breaking your promise are wrong. Even if she does understand she will pretend she doesn't because it's her feelings which are being hurt and it is her who is being betrayed right this minute and nothing else exists in her world at that point but the hurt and disappointment she feels.

She is disappointed mostly in herself rather than in you because it's a big thing these days for a woman to trust a man and that's why we so rarely do. By trusting you we rely on you to keep your word and when you don't we blame ourselves for letting you fool us.

Don't expect us to understand but always tell us why you didn't keep your promise and do it on a date when you didn't and not some time later. When we don't know we make up stories in our heads and these stories are usually not something that makes us feel better but are pretty destructive ones.

For example: "I can't trust him to keep his word! But who am I to ask him anything at all?"

"He didn't keep his promise because he doesn't care about me. He cares more about other things."

"I have to do everything myself! I have no one in the world I can rely on."

Alisa Miller

When we get angry we don't get angry with you. We get angry with ourselves. We get sad and miserable because we feel that suddenly we can't trust the only person we felt we could. We get very aggressive towards you; blaming you now for betraying our trust and not caring about our feelings.

ADVICE
First of all be realistic when you promise something to her. Never make a promise you know you can't keep and if you have the slightest doubt about your ability to keep it make sure she knows there is a possibility that whatever you promised may never happen.

Never give her a date unless you know that will be the actual date when your promise will be kept. And if you still fail to keep your promise never wait for her to understand and move on but always (and I mean it) tell why it didn't happen. We need to hear it from you even if we are quite aware of the situation ourselves.

#26. MARRIAGE: WHY IT IS SO IMPORTANT TO HER

Why re women are so obsessed with marriage? Don't they know that it's just a social contract? That all the promises you men make can be just as easily broken as given and no power on earth can guarantee it will happen otherwise? Yes we do. But it doesn't mean we will stop dreaming and face reality.

You must understand that it is every woman's dream to find the right guy who will take her to a fairy world to live there together happily ever after. And despite the growing numbers of divorces and broken families which recent statistics give us, women still believe that in their case it will be different.

A dream, a perfect picture, a fairy tale that's too tempting to believe in has remained the goal for most women on planet Earth. We get so obsessed with the idea of someone claiming us, saving us from a cruel life of loneliness that pretty much anybody who is willing to do so becomes a prince in our eyes.

It's not the marriage that is so attractive to us but the picture our imagination has drawn in our heads. And although a lot of us with time and experience become sharp and cynical and refuse to follow the same exact pattern our mothers and friends did, it only takes one right guy to break all our prejudices and make us fall in love with the same old dream as everybody else.

But where does it come from? Why do we want you to marry us so much? You may, quite rightly, think that surely, logically, nothing changes after that simple act. But you'll be wrong. Everything changes for both of us. Suddenly you give the ultimate promise to take care of us, "love us tomorrow and forever" no matter what, stay with us for the rest of your life. And I guess this is exactly where most guys have a problem. This ultimate commitment of staying with someone forever, being tied up to one person for the rest of your life and seeing the same face every morning is something few men can actually cope with successfully.

It means no more fishing expeditions to bars, no flirting with every girl you come across, no other woman in your bed but this one. This is a hell of a promise for a man to make and every woman knows that. And this is why it is so important to her that you give that promise.

You see it doesn't take much to make a promise. And even if you believe in it today tomorrow it can be a whole new story. But since marriage is not something you can easily annul overnight it makes it much harder to break and we know that. Plus we always hope that in our case it will be different, that the man we have chosen is different to the rest and has nothing to do with the statistics we hear about in the news.

So marriage plays the kind of seal to the promise you have already made and without it the promise doesn't actually weigh much. Words can be easily given and taken back and every woman knows that.

Alisa Miller

#27. OWNERSHIP

How do you know that something belongs to you? Simple, you just know it. How do other people know that something belongs to you so they can't touch it or make it theirs? You know the answer to that one. When it comes to marriage that's exactly what happens. The question of ownership becomes very clear. Suddenly you have the right, legal right, to say that a woman belongs to you just as well as you belong to her. It's a deal.

Girlfriend, partner, and friend these are all more of a label and don't actually have any value beyond indicating your relation to a woman. But at that point no matter how serious your relationship is it still has no value in eyes of society at large.

You can rebel and say this is why you don't want to marry her, because you feel that it is society that is pushing you and you don't want to give in just because it's something everybody else does. And she will probably agree with you as, quite frankly, she hasn't got any other choice but to do so if she loves you and doesn't want to lose you.

But at the end of the day if you love her "the commitment thing" shouldn't be such a problem. Unless you are not sure in which case it is a different story.

Women are programmed to find a man and form a family, that's what drives us most of the time. And those of us who reject the whole idea of being a slave to nature and follow instinct end up harming ourselves, wallowing in misery and denial.

Sometimes it's too hard to face the truth and we create excuses in order to hide our real feelings and we then start to believe in our own lies.

In fact every woman deeply inside wants to be with a strong man. She may seem hard on the outside, feministic to the tips of her cut-to-the-quick nails but it doesn't come naturally. Deep inside we all want to be owned and treasured and only out of fear of being hurt will we hide our true desires.

Alisa Miller

#28. CRAZY ABOUT HER WEDDING DAY

A woman's wedding day is a special day for her. Some days just are special to all of us but a wedding day has special significance to a woman and it's not something we just made up yesterday ourselves but it goes way back to our ancestors, our roots, the traditions that symbolize the new beginning, the new path you have chosen.

We celebrate our birthdays, we celebrate babies being born, and we celebrate graduation and moving into a new house. The importance of the occasion dictates the scale of the celebration. And how important do you think the wedding day is to a woman who is preparing herself to share the rest of her life with the man she loves? Naturally she'll go mad because, as you would guess she's dreamed about this day and it's finally here and she will try to make it as perfect as it can possibly be.

Although we all know that it's not possible for things to be perfect it doesn't mean she is not going to try. But in this chase for the perfection she needs to achieve on the day she will definitely drive you mad and there is no escaping from that.

Her wedding day for a woman is the day when her dream comes true and the way she feels about it is that it is her day. It is important to her that everything is perfect and that includes you. If you think that every woman's goal is to find a good husband then the wedding is the grand finale of the hunt. Not every one of us of course will admit that but in the end that's all this is about.

To her, her wedding day is something magical and special and a perfect excuse to go mad. It is the day she is the princess in a shiny white dress ready to be rescued by her prince.

ADVICE

The only advice I can give you on this one is to stay cool and bear it. You now can understand why it is so important to her to be your wife and not just a girlfriend or a partner or somebody you just happen to share your bed with. From now on she will be wearing a ring as a proof of being owned by you as well as a new signature with your last name. For many of us it's a new beginning, it's a chance of a new life and a chance of experiencing the happiness we've dreamed about all these years.

Alisa Miller

#29. THE WHITE DRESS

Wedding dresses are expensive and the only reason for them to be so it's because the seller knows the bride will pay for it. It's the must have item for every woman's dream wedding and here is why. Every woman wants to feel special because it's a very special moment in her life and when we are talking about a 200-strong crowd there are only few ways to stand out from it.

A big white dress makes every woman feel like a princess and since it's a dream come true this is how we want to look, like a fairy tale Princess. The bigger the dress the bigger the delight a woman experiences when she is wearing it.

BUT THE TRUTH IS...
There is no real tradition behind a white wedding dress which goes deep in our history. As a matter of fact wearing a special dress has only become a tradition out of fashion set by Queen Victoria in

1840. Before that women used to buy an ordinary dress that they could afterward use as evening dress for special occasions. The idea of a one-time big wedding dress came in after the First World War promoted by wedding caterers and florists, both professions which were generated by jobless professionals searching for new opportunities after the Great War.

So there is no real reason why she has to wear a big white dress or have all these flowers at her wedding. But you need to understand why she feels she needs to have it all. She wants to feel like a Princess and if you can afford for her to feel that way, well, she is a very lucky girl.

UNDER PRESSURE
We women are constantly under pressure to find a man and make him marry us and each one of us has our own reasons and motives for doing so. Some of us want to start a family with the right guy, some of us are simply trying to secure our future and most of us are waiting for mister Perfect. The majority of us will settle for much less as soon as we hit the critical age and sense that time is against us.

You see a woman has to have a mate, someone to take care of her and her offsprings. Naturally we are guided by nature to find the strongest and the best and make him settle with us. But it's not just the pressure of a biological drive we are under here but the pressure from society as well.

We know that each day we are not getting any younger. Our chances to find the right guy are getting smaller and smaller every year so naturally we are constantly under tremendous pressure from every front to find a man and settle down with him as soon as we can.

So, here is why we feel the urge more than you do: We want children. Never mind the fact that our biological clock is ticking and our fertility is not getting any better, but there is always the fear that we will not have a father for our children.

Every woman knows that it takes two to raise a child and unless there is no other choice the man, the father and the provider is on the must-have list and everything else is optional.

Our parents and friends constantly push us. It's just like we don't feel bad enough already when we haven't found a partner at a certain age; when our mum or dad would start to publicly humiliate us with "Haven't you found a husband yet?" It's normal for them to worry as they are afraid that there will be no one around to take care of us when they are gone. But it doesn't help us much when they constantly get on our cases over that.

Love speculation in the media. We see everywhere pictures of happy couples and romantic movies with happy endings and we start to imagine ourselves having a family just like that. Essentially we associate marriage with a magic pill of instant happiness. And although most of us will probably understand how silly these thoughts are the pill promises too much for us to at least try it.

But most of all we are just afraid of staying alone for the rest of our life, getting old and never being able to find a man we can spend it with. The pressure never goes away even if we cut out the phone calls and stop visiting our parents at Christmas and turn off the TV, there will still be no one to hug us at night.

#30. WHY DOES SHE GET FAT AFTER MARRIAGE?

I've heard a lot of husbands' complaints about their wives putting weight on after the marriage and it always makes me raise my eyebrows.

As you can see keeping in shape for a woman is a huge struggle and the only reason she does that it's because she needs you to be attracted to her. If your wife gets fat after the marriage that means that she has finally relaxed and let herself go. The entire struggle we go through is actually for you to commit and after that most of us finally relax about our looks. Not very wise from my point of view but that's how it normally works for most of us.

Alisa Miller

As time passes she gets tired of constantly saying no to the things you eat for example. I call it a "companion eating" effect. She serves you things she knows you like but when you will easily burn it all off she simply can't. So the only way for her to keep in shape is to eat different things and much smaller amount to the ones you are having. And this is not as easy as it sounds. She will feel left out and you will think she is weird. But as we are going against nature with a regime designed to keep us thin through small food portions there is no easy way of doing it. It's either having a fat-free yogurt when you are having grilled chicken or getting fat. If your wife is beginning to put on weight after marriage you know what she has chosen then.

ADVICE
You can make it easier for her and help her keep in shape at the same time. It will not be easy for you through because it requires you to not just support her dieting but at least visually diet with her. Try to stick with the eating times and have meals together and encourage her to cook healthy low-fat meals for both of you (you can snack with junk food all you want as long as she doesn't see it).

You can try buying her expensive clothes one size smaller then she is but it only works if she really likes what you bought for her and she the tries to lose weight in order to wear it.

Then again she needs to feel that keeping in shape is worth it if she feels you don't really care about her looks she won't bother. Inspire her and show understanding when she diets and praise her with non-food related gifts to make her feel attractive.

If you need her to go on a diet don't just tell her that. It's too easy to hurt her feelings and make her get depressed as she will feel that you think she is fat and she'll probably find comfort in a dozen cupcakes making things even worse. Tell her that you are going on a diet yourself and would she want to join you in an adventure and that approach may just work. Joining the gym together, changing your lifestyle together can work very nicely if you want her to be more aware of her body.

But the main problem with her getting fat is usually in her self-image. A woman would really try hard not to get there in the first place if she feels she still needs to be attractive. If you don't pay attention to her and her looks, if you don't tell her you love her body she has no reason to keep it trim.

Alisa Miller

#31. WHY DO WOMEN WANT KIDS?

A lot of women want to have children because they see it as fulfilling their biological destiny - to become a mother and give their man a child.

It is part of our programming as a species to multiply and it's natural that at some point a woman wants to experience motherhood. We see a child as an extension of our love, something that our love gives birth to when you normally see it as a very expensive whim. We find children, our children beautiful because they are the mix of two people who belong to each other creating the ultimate connection between them. Most of us want to have a child by the man we love so we can see that man in a child and that way extend our feelings.

The whole experience of motherhood fascinates us. We feel the need to try it and fill our life with a purpose. Yet a lot of us don't really know why we do want kids and probably won't be able to explain it. There are two common reasons women would want to have a child: First, we feel that is what we are supposed to do right after we find the right man. Second, we feel this is the only way we can have someone love us unconditionally.

Years ago before the Pill it was impossible to have sex and not get pregnant so giving birth was something every woman was destined to do and not just once but, usually, quite a few time sin her lifetime.

Since then a lot of things have changed and now while having full control of our body's fertility as women we still want to have children. Apart from being programmed by nature to find a partner and mate in order to have offspring we also follow the example of other women surrounding us and without this example it would be very different in our minds.

Imagine if for example, men could give birth, you in particular, and other men around you would have children and you didn't. Wouldn't you be curious what it is like to have a child? And every woman is fascinated by the idea of becoming a mother and have someone she could dedicate her life to and who will love her in return.

We want to have a child and care for it to see it grow up and develop. We want to make a human being and do it right. Sometimes we want to live though our children and sometimes we want to fill our own life with meaning so suddenly we would have someone to take care of most of our time. As an idea it always sounds good in our heads. Unfortunately it doesn't always work out the way we expect.

Alisa Miller

We normally see all the good sides of motherhood, fantastic pictures from movies and heart touching moments in books and magazines. We always see our child being perfect and loving us for the rest of his (or her) life. We think more about the names or colors we going to use for the nursery then we think about all the drawbacks and sacrifices we will have to make in order to bring them up. And even if you point them all out to us we will always reply: "It's going to be different with us".

But it's not all fluff 100% of the time. A lot of us also understand that having a child doesn't only mean having an ultimate connection with you but having a connection for the rest of your life. We understand you will (probably) never leave a child and translate it into "you will never leave us". Some women get pregnant on purpose to tie you to them. And in case of one child growing up too fast we will have two or three just in case. So even if you leave us then we will be financially secure anyway.

#32. SEX : HOW IMPORTANT IS IT FOR HER?

The question of sex is a question which can have many answers but I will, in this case, be a little more absolute than usual: Sex, for a woman, depends on the quality of her relationship full stop.

You see good sex is only a vital must-have for a woman if the relationship is not so good. But normally that kind of relationship doesn't last. So the truth is no, sex is not that important for a woman. If she will have to choose between good sex and a good relationship she would choose the last one every time. You see the emotional side is much more important to her than the physical one and having a good relationship with you is more important to her than having fantastic sex.

Women can have sex and read a book at the same time. You would think we would feel quite a lot but we don't, unless we want to. If our head is busy with something else and you are, well, not making an effort yourself we won't probably feel anything at all.

Unlike you most of us don't need an orgasm every day. We are quite happy to have it once or twice a week and at the end of the day we can help ourselves if we need to. That's why we are quite happy to provide the service if you need it but don't make a big deal out of it. So even if we are not in the mood we will still do it for you. Why? Because it's not a big deal and in most cases it doesn't even last that long.

Provided we are happy with you we will try to please you but not ourselves when it comes to sex. We will never jeopardize our good relationship because we didn't orgasm last week. It doesn't mean we won't let you know if the sex is bad. But the better the relationship the lower the chances you will ever find out if there is a problem on the sex front.

Priority wise sex comes second but if the relationship sucks you'll be first to know that she is dissatisfied on the sex front. Or if she feels she can't talk to you about it and she can't find the courage to leave you she will find somebody else to have sex with because she then needs to fill the emotional vacuum with something, anything.

How do we feel when we have sex? It feels good but only if we let it to feel good and the more predictable it is the easier it becomes to feel less and less with time. That's why a lot of couples try to find new things to do during sex. But the secret is: it's not in the technique.

Sex for a woman is not down there, as everything else in her life, sex is in her head. In order to feel something she has to be excited in the first place. She needs to want you and feel passionate about you and what you are doing. Otherwise she may just as well watch TV while you are doing whatever you need to do in order to orgasm.

Alisa Miller

#33. WHY DOES SHE FAKE ORGASM AND HOW TO FIND OUT IF SHE DOES?

There can be many excuses which I could use here to make you feel better but we have been open and honest so far so let's continue in this vein. We fake orgasms because we can.

You see most of us simply can't orgam every time we have sex but we feel you expect us to. While you are ready pretty much any time for sex, sex for us is something we have to be ready for emotionally.

Small things can stop us from enjoying the act and the worst of it we can't control it. To enjoy sex we need to be completely relaxed and not every woman can actually do that. Some women go through life without having a single orgasm because they simply can't relax. It can be anything at all which prevents from relaxing, from small to big things, from problems at work to a tap dripping in the bathroom and it takes a lot of patience if you want to get us excited when we are feeling tense.

On the other hand we can just fake an orgasm and get on with our day keeping you happy at the same time. It becomes so convenient that at some point women stop even trying to enjoy sex with their partners. They just lie there and "think of England" for a while waiting for you to finish. And this kind of thing is not as rare as you might think and probably at least few girls have done it with you.

If we like the guy, better still, if we love him, we will do anything to please him. We will do things we don't really want to do just to keep him happy. After all it's not like it hurts or even requires us to exert ourselves physically, for that you are the one who is doing most of the action anyway.

HOW TO FIND OUT IF SHE IS FAKING

I remember all those articles over the net in the early stages of the web when everyone went online just for one thing and one thing only: either to find sex or find out about sex.

There were lots of articles on how to spot if she faked orgasm or not. They mentioned a certain pigmentation of the skin on her chest as physical evidence. But unless your particular girl has some serious skin problem this is not how you can tell, I can assure you. In fact there is no easy way for you to tell if she had an orgasm or if she faked it unless she really wants you to know.

Women can experience two types of orgasms: clitoral and vaginal. Both of these are good but different and to achieve each one of these you apply different techniques. Some of us are just generally more sensitive than others and having a vaginal orgasm with a guy will be easier without him trying very hard. But you need to really fit very well with each other or the girl has to be really gifted naturally and can experience an orgasm at the first touch. The rest of us, the majority in fact, need hard work in order to orgasm.

It is only fair to examine here when it's harder for us to experience an orgasm.

When we are very tired or close to exhaustion.

When we are stressed and our mind is preoccupied with something else.

When we are not feeling well. Do bear in mind that when it comes to headaches studies have shown that sex is actually a cure because it helps lower the blood pressure.

A vaginal orgasm is not as strong as a clitoral one and you will know the difference if you will ever give your partner one. And this is one of the reasons why identifying if she had an orgasm is so difficult because in the case of vaginal orgasms you may feel the inner muscles of the vaginal canal vibrate, but you could also not feel a thing even if you made her fly to the moon while with the clitoral orgasm you will be sure 100% she is not faking it because she will be almost out of control.

So what's better for her to experience, a clitoral or a vaginal orgasm? Well, it's just different there is no 'better'. A clitoral orgasm may feel much stronger and lasts longer while a vaginal orgasm could feel more fulfilling. But as long as she had one it counts just the same.

The reason you can't really tell if she had an orgasm is because there are no physical signs as such although in the case of the clitoral orgasm her clitoris will be very sensitive for a minute or so and she will shiver or move away from your hand.

Also you can probably judge according to the way she behaves after the act. A woman who just had an orgasm won't try and have sex with you right away. Most women wouldn't want to have sex after having an orgasm at all.

But no matter how hard you try to read the signs you can never be absolutely sure unless it's as obvious as her snoring after you've finished.

Alisa Miller

#34. DOES SHE MASTURBATE?

Masturbation is a perfectly normal expression of female sexuality just as it is of male sexuality. Most women do masturbate frequently. Masturbation is the same for both sexes it's the way we can relax and let go at least for a few minutes. No one can know how to give you pleasure so well as you can do it for yourself. Plus there is no commitment or small talk afterwards. In many cases masturbation can be much better than actual sex with your partner; the orgasm can be more intensive and faster to reach. But it's never the same thing although the orgasm is the same the general experience isn't. When a woman has sex with someone she loves or at least likes she experiences something much more precious to her then having an orgasm: closeness. And a lot of us would agree to have no orgasm at all but have this sense of closeness which we cannot experience through masturbation alone.

So have no illusions women do masturbate just as often as men do and the orgasms we have might be even more intense and fulfilling then yours. Who can understand us better then we understand ourselves and our bodies? This is why it is so tricky for a man to become a good lover to a woman who is already a perfect lover to herself.

WHERE AND HOW?
When it comes to masturbation women are no different to men, we can have sex anywhere, anytime. But bearing in mind our physiology we do need a private space as panties have to come off. Some women are luckier then others and their sensitivity is extreme so they can orgasm much faster and with less trouble. But others need a quite room or at least a bathroom with running water.

Anything can be used for masturbation as for us, women, it's nothing more than stimulation most of the time. Hard objects may also be used, depending on what kind of orgasm we want to experience clitoral or vaginal or both.

A vaginal orgasm can only be reached with the use of a dildo-like object or the intense stimulation provided by a good, strong horse-ride, for example, (or the much more accessible, mechanical simulation of one). For a woman sex is all in her head. Can we orgasm without any stimulation at all by just getting turned on too much? It's unlikely. But fantasizing will make us orgasm the moment the clitoris gets any kind of stimulation at all. That's why foreplay is so important for a woman as sex always starts in her head and then ends up in her pants.

Most women prefer clitoral stimulation because it's a fast and easy way to have a good orgasm. We learn how to masturbate when we are little girls getting excited and rubbing between our legs. A woman would never forget an orgasm. So if she is not sure if she ever had one that means she didn't.

WHAT'S THE TRICK?
For her sex always starts in her head. So if you fail to turn her on up there you will fail to do it further south. You see just sex on its own does nothing for her and she can just as well read a book in the process. Eventually if you do go on for hours she will make up a story in her head on her own and have an orgasm but if you are a fast runner and you didn't make sure she is already about to come before you even started she probably won't even try to do it herself.

Compared to sex which, inevitably, takes place in her body, masturbation is always about what's in her head that's why for most women it is so good. Unlike you we are not so visually-led and barely get excited looking at your genitals unless we are really into yours particularly. We get turned on playing a movie in our head with the scenarios we find exciting. For every woman it's something she finds hot and it can be something she would never want to experience in real life.

Masturbation is something we all do but we don't want other people to know about it. It's personal and very sacred and women are more likely to keep quite about it when men are about. Well, when other women are about too. Discretion here is very part of the female make up which is why sometimes guys wonder if women masturbate at all.

WHAT WOMEN FANTASIZE ABOUT WHEN MUSTARBATING?

When we masturbate we fantasize about anything we find sexy. It can be harmless things like having sex on a plane or in a public place. We can replay moments from movies that excited us or make up a moment we thought would be exciting enough to happen with a particular character.

We can be pretty sick in our fantasies but it doesn't mean we would ever consider trying something like that in real life. For example rape fantasies are pretty common but a real is something no woman would want to ever happen to her, it's the kind of thing which works only as a fantasy.

Even when a woman is fantasizing about someone she knows it's always more about the story than about the act itself. Sometimes a woman can come just playing the scenario in her head and masturbating and never even reaching the final stage of the sex-act itself.

But in general we are very much like you when it comes to giving ourselves pleasure. Whatever turns us on, we do. Our fantasies are often reflected by our upbringing, character and our environment. Some women like men in uniforms and play different scenarios about having sex at their workplace or seducing them. Others like to have fantasies about forbidden things depending on what they feel is forbidden to them. But we all have one thing in common when it comes to sexual fantasies: it's not the who it's the where and how.

Alisa Miller

#35. DOES SHE LIKE PORN?

Most women do like porn but they won't tell you that. Porn is a bad word and every little girl knows that. It's like those other taboo words: 'fuck' or 'fart'. Good girls just don't use words like that. And if we really like you we will make ourselves at least appear to be good.

As a matter of fact porn turns women on more then it does men. And women living on their own will probably have a porn collection just as big as yours. But if she is in a relationship she is more likely to have no porn around at all in case you will find it. And for a woman it's like being caught masturbating.

So when it comes to talking about it she will probably rather not discuss it which wouldn't mean at all that she doesn't like it. Some things are better kept private.

Porn acts like a switch to the right mood and for a woman it's not something easily accomplished in any other way. Women are too preoccupied with problems and every day worries to be able to just relax and let it go. When watching porn we don't think about anything else and that's why it's the ultimate way to distance ourselves from the whole world and concentrate on our sexuality.

PORN, YOU AND HER
The problem with the word 'porn' is that like all other four letter words 'love', 'work' and 'poem' included, the moment it is mentioned a lot of what I would call 'reason' goes flying out the figurative window and we are left to deal with a whole lot of kneejerk reactions which rely upon emotion, hearsay and prejudice to work.

Andrea Dworkin, the anti-porn activist, rose to fame in the 1980s arguing that if we did not limit pornography most men would objectify women more intensively and treat them less as people than as porn stars. The floodgates would open; rape and other sexual transgressions would follow. Her tirade perhaps reflected a whole lot of her own misconceptions and the fact that we live in a world where the objectification of women in the mass media and advertising and the mainstream acceptance of porn have not led to an all-out explosion of mass rapes and sexual transgressions perhaps suggests that Dworkin was not as right as she thought.

She did however have a point which most people miss and I will change the word porn here for hamburger. Suppose you could have a hamburger whenever you wanted, any time of the day, at any moment, any day of the week, all year round, until the end of time, without having to worry about getting fat. For some people that might be their idea

Alisa Miller

of heaven. They may well end up eating six Big Macs in the first half of the day alone. They may, even, finish the day with another six and they might repeat this the very next day.

Hamburgers, or junk food for that matter, can be addictive because they feed the pleasure center of the brain more than the stomach. Like an addiction they soon produce an effect known as habituation. This means that the pleasure eating a hamburger would produce begins to drop off as we eat more and more, more and more frequently and we then begin to require stronger and stronger tastes or more exotic ones in order to get the same buzz out of it.

This is the one valid, logically-sound argument against porn, or rather against the excessive use of porn. Watching it, on your own, or with a partner is great as a source of inspiration, a means to get ideas, a way to elicit excitement and experimentation. It is also great as a way of widening the horizons of your sexual experience and the possibilities this raises. Overdo it however and you get trapped in an endless cycle of diminishing pleasure and increased need for stimulation. This will not only affect your own viewing habits when it comes to porn but it will also begin to affect the quality of your real-life sexual relationships.

It is exactly at this junction that porn begins to get bad for a relationship. Is this bad enough to call for legislation and legal controls of pornography? Probably not, even if we assume that most men and women are not mature enough or disciplined enough to control their porn consumption. We can however, and perhaps we should, provide adequate sexual education and encourage an atmosphere of openness and objectivity in which the likes of Dworkin find it hard going to make a case.

Then and only then will we succeed in having the best of all worlds. A place where porn is enjoyed for what it is, sexuality is accepted without taboos and limits have more to do with self-regulation and common sense rather than morality.

When it comes to you and her and porn the answer is everything is permitted provided no one gets hurt and it does not damage your relationship. Explore it with a partner you are really into and who is really into you and it becomes a mind-blowing experience where the on-screen action is dwarfed in scope and excitement by the off-screen action.

As always, you need to explore this with sensitivity and mutual respect for each other's needs and boundaries.

Alisa Miller

#36. DOES SIZE MATTER TO HER?

If we judge by the number of spam emails we get each day we'd be forgiven for thinking that the world's male population is suffering from stunted penises and spend their entire day looking for ways to rectify the problem in order to get a woman.

Size is not as much an issue for a woman as you think. You may believe that surely size of man's penis matters as at the end of the day as a woman wants to feel something inside her this is only partially true. When it comes to sex size is the last thing in a woman's mind (unless her partner is so well endowed that it becomes a challenge fitting in).

Usually the issue of 'size' is something which men are preoccupied with. If you think it is an issue and you talk about it with your partner you will always find a solution no matter what the perceived problem might be. If you really want to make your relationship work you will do it. Pretending that nothing is wrong only makes things worse as it accumulates inside on partner's head and eventually becomes an issue which will 'explode'. A woman won't be extremely happy with a man who not only doesn't just have a penis sufficiently large to do the job but us also unwilling to talk about it – she sees that as a partner who is ignoring her needs.

If you are not big enough for her all it shows is that you will need to compensate for it differently. You see a woman would not complain much if a man is simply not good in bed but everything is fine with his size as subconsciously she will also look for a problem in herself. But she surely will blame you if she can't even feel you inside her never mind experiencing an orgasm.

So what can you do if size is really an issue? First of all acknowledge it. A lot of men simply can't admit that their penis is not big enough to satisfy a woman. They blame the statistics, porn movies, the woman they are with and her oversized vagina but never themselves.

Step one – realize that there is nothing to be ashamed of as it happens naturally. Second do realize that it does require action and not denial. Third, work with your partner to solve this for both of you.

It might be worth it here to ask, what's the average penis size then? According to the latest research the average penis length (when erect) is from 5.1 inches to 5.7 inches (12.9 cm to 14.5 cm).

Unfortunately much as men worry about their size no matter how big they are it's not the size which gives us, women, pleasure. Even if you have an oversized giant that doesn't mean you know how to use it. A lot of men think that all they've got to do is just 'stick it in there' and she will instantly come. But it doesn't happen so easily unless a woman is already about to orgasm.

To give her pleasure if you are really interested in doing so takes more then just in-and-out for 5 minutes. Sex for a woman is always in her head and if you have failed to arouse here there nothing is going to happen in the place where the physical action is.

She needs to be in the right mood, she needs to be excited and free from daily worries, she needs to want you and she needs her foreplay.

If you learn what your particular woman likes, what she wants, how she wants it the penis size won't play much of a role. After all there are other ways to give her pleasure. You just need to ask her, talk about it and you both will be happy.

#37. SEX VS CUDDLING

This is a purely female thing you need to know as a guy. You see for us, women, cuddling and sex are two different things. We can just cuddle and never take it any further because it's the cuddling we actually enjoy and at that particular time we don't even think about sex. We feel very relaxed and peaceful and we treasure this time with you because for us it's ultimate intimacy where you are concentrated on us and us only.

Normally we think that everything you always think of has to do with sex. Every time you grab us we feel that it's all you want from us. And most of the time we are probably right. We get upset if you want too much sex from us and we get upset when you don't want it enough. So finding just the right way to behave around us is very tricky but is very important.

Alisa Miller

Unlike you we don't need sex (or rather we don't feel like it) every time you lay your hands on us. We like you to want us and we like you being gentle and we really enjoy this time. We will go ahead having sex with you if we feel that this is what you really need right now but for us it will be something we are doing for you and not the logical end result of the cuddling.

This is a significant distinction in the psychological make-up of men and women. For a woman, cuddling, touching and kissing is every bit as important as the bump and grind of sex is to a man.

#38. HOW TO BRING HER OFF

There is an important thing you need to understand when it comes to sex. Just having the right tools doesn't make you the master of the sex act itself, Being able to use them right does. There are different ways to give a woman pleasure and it doesn't necessary include your penis all the time.

We, women, are funny creatures. We would rather wait for you to finish and never experience an orgasm during the sex act itself but would not tell you straight what we would like you to do to us so we can orgasm too. We don't do it on purpose, we just don't feel comfortable telling you about it and you can even say we are shy. So the only way to get to the bottom of it (literally) is to stimulate us and make us give up all the secrets along the way.

The most sensitive thing in a woman's body is her clitoris. But it's a very sensitive, even fragile part of her body and just going in there like a caveman handling things roughly is not a good idea and it only happens in the movies. When it comes to her body you need to have more patience and dedication than you might even think is possible.

For a woman sex is always in her head and there is only a small percentage of the process which, for her, is physical, right at the end. You've probably heard before (and I've already mentioned it here) that a lot of us can't orgasm because we simply can't relax. And it's true, but it's not exactly the way it sounds. In order to relax a woman needs to trust a man she is with completely in order to lose her guard and this is where even long-term partners fail sometimes. The way a woman relates to sex is complicated and unlike you we can't just let go unless we are ready for it.

There are some things you should know before you even start: First of all make sure you are ready to go to the end if you start. We will be disappointed although we probably won't tell you that. Make sure we are excited before you even take her clothes off. There is nothing worse for her than having sex with you when her head is busy with other things. It can be things she has planned, a movie she has watched or anything at all. Make sure she is responding to your affection – she kisses you back, she bends her body, she touches you. It's a good start.

Next, be patient and don't rush. The longer you tease her - the easier it will be to bring her off.

Don't rush to her clitoris straight away. She needs time to turn her body on and be prepared physically. Unless you are using the lube the minimum cuddling time for her to be able to produce vaginal liquid is up to 5-10 minutes depending on her physiology and her level of excitement. Touch her very gently down there and make sure she is wet before you do anything at all. If she isn't keep kissing her and touching her erogenous zones (providing you know them – it can be any part of her body – ears, spine, her palms any part she reacts the most when you touch it). If you try to rub her clitoris when it's not wet it can actually hurt and put her off sex at that point (and again she probably won't tell you that – we, women, are not very big on explaining how we feel about sex during sex if you don't seize the initiative and ask).

Use lube or your own saliva if you don't want to wait. But saliva doesn't have the same properties as natural liquid or lube. It's not oily enough so be aware of that. She won't feel as good when you touch her down there when the liquid is not oily. It just makes it feel alright and you can freely touch her there without being afraid to hurt her. So the main thing you need to remember: she needs to be wet before you move to the next stage. Oily wet preferably.

Stimulation is the key. You probably heard that before. We, women, know our body very well and yet we can't always bring ourselves off if we are tense. So we don't expect you to be the hero of the day 100% of the time. Investing your time and energy into learning and trying to give us pleasure means a lot to us and there is a risk she will try and make you think you have already done it because we simply don't want you to suffer and wait for us forever. That's when she will fake it. And we pretend we do it for you when in reality we do it so we don't have to fight ourselves and concentrate on teaching you how to do it right.

I know learning to pleasure a woman's body is a long process but it's worth it and in order to be able to do it any time, be in control of our body, you will probably have to fight her first. But then it only gets better.

All you need to do is stimulate her clitoris with your finger very, very, very slowly. Make circular movement around the tip of it, sliding on its oily surface. You will know you are doing well if she will start slowly moving in time with your stimulating her and even start moaning. Her skin will start getting warmer. Make sure she is in a comfortable position as things can take time and you don't want her to get numb half way through because she has not been positioned properly.

I'll let you in on a secret: We are all different physiologically but some things are the same for all of us. The wider her legs are spread the more intense the experience. And if you open the petals of her clitoris during the stimulation you are onto a winner here. She is more likely to reach the boiling point faster if you do just that.

Once you get her going and moving and moaning all you need to do is move faster listening carefully to her breathing. You will know if she is ready if she will start being anxious. At the pick of the climax we, women, become indifferent to anything surrounding us and just let it all go. At that point we are very dangerous creatures. We want nothing more than to orgasm. So we'll probably kick you if you stop. So just keep going and you will know we have climaxed if we start screaming or push you away, or our hands turn into claws on your back.

One way or another we will let you know and it will be quite visual that we have just experienced clitoral orgasm. At that point we don't want you to touch it anymore for another minute or so. It becomes very sensitive and over-stimulation becomes uncomfortable.

Here is another big secret: If you use your penis instead of the finger the experience might be even better for both you and your partner, especially if you enter her right at the point of her orgasm and you manage to climax together.

Alisa Miller

#39. WHAT DOES SHE FANTASIZE ABOUT?

You would probably run far away from her in you knew what this sensitive fragile flower of yours is fantasizing about when you are not around (and even when you are). Sex, for a woman, always starts in her head and then travels further south and having VARIOUS fantasies is what keeps it exciting for her.

Most of us have tried pretty much everything sexual when it comes to fantasizing but it doesn't mean that we actually ever want these fantasies to come true.

Shockingly, she could have had (and some even argue, should have had) all sorts of fantasies you would only know about going through the wickedest pages of Wikipedia. Her healthy sense of curiosity and the safest sex in the world (masturbation) really open doors to the use (and abuse) of her imagination.

And I am not talking, here, about plumbers and movie stars. What fascinates us is novelty and safe violence. Fantasies of rape or sex with aliens could be one of these things she wouldn't mind exploring especially knowing that she would never actually let something like this happen willingly with her in real life. The world of women's sexual fantasies is not something she actually wants to happen, it's pretty much the total opposite to yours, this is something that can never happen and some women find it exciting. We get bored and we make up stories and we enjoy the game.

The other thing we do is fantasize about someone we know. Sex itself does very little for us if there is no scenario to excite our mind. So even if we fantasize about an actor or a friend it will all go back to the storyline we would enjoy with anyone else just as much it's just this time it happens to be this particular person.

Any cliché scenario suddenly can become new and exciting if we change the face of a character or the circumstances where it all takes place.

She can have fantasies, for example, about making up for a parking ticket or having sex with her boss but the sex part is not what is going to excite her. What really does it for her is the foreplay and the seduction process itself. It's all about perfect control in an environment she can't really get in real life. And even if you try and recreate it for her it won't as perfect as she has painted it using her imagination. On the other hand, why would you? We know what you dream about. We leave you with your world alone, and we deserve a little privacy in ours, in return.

Alisa Miller

ABOUT THE AUTHOR

Alisa Miller, has lived in three countries and two continents. A former model she has used her training to focus on relationship issues and her first book, 'Ultimate Guide to the Perfect Relationship' became an internet phenomenon appearing both as an eBook and on paper all over the web in the first week of publication. She has, since, written for hundreds of websites and magazines. She edited a magazine and has been working hard on more books in the dating, sex and relationships areas. She runs her own website and spends more time online than even she admits is healthy.

Other books by the same author

Alisa Miller's books are available to buy from every major bookstore on both sides of the Atlantic. They can be bought online at Amazon.com plus a large number of established online book retailers.

They are also available as downloads for Amazon Kindle, the Sony eBook reader and smartphones and PDAs from Mobipocket.com and any large online eBook retailer.

Alisa Miller

Stay current

The author is active in the content of her own website which is updated on an almost daily basis. Apart from articles on relationships, real-life stories and the author's own Blog her website: www.alisa-miller.com is also the place where you can find her latest publications at a discounted price.

The author also maintains a Facebook Fan page where she interacts with her fans regularly and messages all those who join once a week:

To join the author's fan page go to:
http://www.facebook.com/Miller.Alisa

www.ingramcontent.com/pod-product-compliance
Lightning Source LLC
LaVergne TN
LVHW051123080426
835510LV00018B/2201